# The Big 11+

# Word Power

# Book

## Pathway to Success

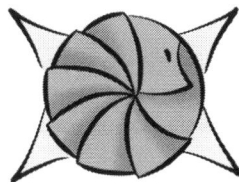

The Armadillo's Pillow Ltd

**ISBN  978-1-912936-13-7**

71-75 Shelton Street
Covent Garden
London, England, WC2H 9JQ
United Kingdom

# The Big 11+ Word Power Book

## Contents

# The Big 11+ Word Power Book

## Contents

# PATHWAY TO SUCCESS
## 11+ Word Power

Designed to complement *The Big 11+ Vocabulary Play Book*, this collection of exercises concentrates on continued improvement of vocabulary and verbal reasoning skills. With a variety of different problem types, these have been created to help improve performance on the Eleven Plus exam, independent school exams, Year 6 SATS, and other English tests.

The worksheets include variations of verbal reasoning questions including cloze problems, jumbled sentences, synonyms and antonyms, as well as other exercises such as Odd One Out and letter codes. The last section is a review of tricky spellings, this comprises the words that are the most frequently misspelt or used incorrectly.

At varying points, your child may run into a word they do not know. Use this as an opportunity to write it down and learn the new vocabulary. Although it is not necessary to time each section, we have provided a suggested completion time and level of difficulty. Keep in mind the Eleven Plus exam is a timed test.

In the Armadillo's Pillow style, we have included some puns, puzzles and humorous illustrations to help make sure the learning does not get too stale. These sections have been labelled 'Just For Fun,' to provide some added interest, but also reinforce vocabulary and word association.

We hope that this book will help your child to continue to improve their performance in whatever exam they are sitting, and encourage greater enthusiasm in their further educational and life endeavours.

Elizabeth Judge
The Armadillo's Pillow Ltd

# Synonym Pairs 1
Difficulty Level: Easy
(Suggested completion time: 10 minutes)

---

Select the two words, one from each group, that are the <u>closest</u> in meaning.

*.Example:*        (throw quit jump)     (stop quick stand)

*Answer:* **quit stop**

---

1)        (amount bend sleep)    (throw blow measure)

2)        (company edge forest)    (tear business wing)

3)        (cane harbour shed)    (valley look quay)

4)        (flap frog foe)    (pond friend enemy)

5)        (sly angry shy)    (silly dangerous crafty)

6)        (brave hostile brief)    (long wide short)

7)        (propel guarantee delay)    (promise neglect bury)

8)        (deadly careful fattening)    (fleet agile fatal)

9)        (optimum obvious oblong)    (apparent adult aggravate)

10)        (upset mercy patience)    (oddity creativity forgiveness)

11)        (sphere rectangle bag)    (orb bottle garb)

12)        (hamlet orchestra catastrophe)    (pamphlet operation disaster)

13)        (enormous elegant fake)    (simple stylish realistic)

14)        (lotion slice beverage)    (spray drink container)

15)        (original dingy frozen)    (authentic stingy changing)

# Synonym Pairs 2

Difficulty Level: Medium

(Suggested completion time: 10 minutes)

Select the two words, one from each group, that are the closest in meaning.

1) (hoax  coax  treat)  (cloak  trick  folk)

2) (comical  clever  coy)  (bright  sad  eager)

3) (throw  curb  lead)  (restrain  follow  reach)

4) (profit  withdraw  money)  (order  gain  balance)

5) (door  continue  depart)  (arrive  exit  travel)

6) (charming  evasive  polite)  (savoury  sweet  tangy)

7) (modest  abundant  curious)  (dearth  adequate  plenty)

8) (refuse  repair  release)  (fail  detain  deny)

9) (routine  honourable  hearty)  (distinguished  competent  resolved)

10) (fatigue  intensity  stamina)  (punctuality  reluctance  weariness)

11) (flat  rough  bouncy)  (uneven  level  floor)

12) (adequate  hollow  pungent)  (broad  uncertain  void)

13) (endeavour  limit  acquire)  (relocate  obtain  disperse)

14) (admission  ticket  confirmation)  (revelation  track  exclusion)

15) (branch  trench  crevice)  (root  limb  trunk)

# Synonym Pairs 3

Difficulty Level: Medium/Hard

(Suggested completion time: 10 minutes)

Select the two words, one from each group, that are the closest in meaning.

1) (wander  employ  frequent)   (engage  discard  negotiate)

2) (box  excavate  bolster)   (maintain  create  dig)

3) (opaque  discerning  clear)   (loose  apparent  scary)

4) (sew  embellish  pattern)   (remove  decorate  button)

5) (futile  abundant  encouraged)   (future  scarce  hopeless)

6) (sensitive  severe  sincere)   (harsh  fantastic  vague)

7) (nonchalant  intrigued  dismissive)   (careful  casual  academic)

8) (din  chaos  banter)   (serenity  league  disarray)

9) (summit  base  station)   (boulder  peak  mountain)

10) (unpredictable  slow  direct)   (constant  erratic  stable)

11) (musical  contrary  confined)   (opposite  custodial  similar)

12) (brief  abrupt  unfriendly)   (apologetic  lame  concise)

13) (coarse  sleek  loose)   (shiny  porous  obstinate)

14) (vacant  holiday  occupied)   (wide  angled  empty)

15) (crash  tumult  summersault)   (uproar  peace  complaint)

# Synonym Pairs 4

Difficulty Level: Hard

(Suggested completion time: 12 minutes)

Select the word on the right that is the closest in meaning to the word in **bold** on the left.

*Example:*   **big**      small   (large)   medium   tiny   less

Answer:      **large**

1) **ambition**    lethal    credit    ambivalent    desire    liberty    amber

2) **heist**    heroine    rescue    stage    theft    accomplice    bridge

3) **jester**    nonsense    wit    puppet    magician    foul    folly    crop

4) **pioneer**    traitor    tyrant    tenant    innovator    candidate    worker

5) **bountiful**    bouncy    scarce    genuine    dubious    meager    abundant

6) **indulge**    pamper    interrogate    insert    enter    prefer    pardon

7) **temporary**    prompt    superb    enduring    lethargic    brief    slight

8) **precise**    sluggish    tolerant    exact    approximately    rapid    extra

9) **restore**    revoke    blame    remedy    remain    recite    purchase

10) **wise**    arrogant    elegant    cordial    astute    reckless    uninformed

11) **diminish**    bargain    impose    increase    transfer    decrease

12) **vain**    sane    conceited    shy    worried    artery    weather

13) **vast**    dainty    steep    shady    extensive    expensive    solid

14) **crucial**    colonial    culinary    cruel    critical    loud    cantankerous

15) **perish**    flourish    pursue    die    submit    endure    evacuate    peril

# Synonym Matching
Difficulty Level: Medium/Hard
(Suggested completion time: 10 minutes)

Match the word on the left with the word that has the closest meaning on the right column.

| | |
|---|---|
| variety | connection |
| section | advance |
| resemble | massive |
| excitement | rupture |
| link | scrub |
| scour | hysteria |
| burst | mirror |
| tremendous | accept |
| generic | swerve |
| veer | assortment |
| progress | common |
| agree | slice |

# JUST FOR FUN
## *Spiral Word Puzzle*

Use the clues to answer the words, which go in a clockwise spiral. Note: The <u>first</u> letter of each word is the <u>last</u> letter of the previous word.

| 1 | Q | | E | | U | | 2 T |
|---|---|---|---|---|---|---|---|
| | | I | | 7 N | | V | |
| R | | O | 11 | | U | 8 | R |
| | S | | N | | T | A | R |
| P | | M | E | | | | N |
| | | 12 | | | C | H | N |
| V | 10 E | | T | | U | 9 | 3 |
| 6 | K | | 5 | E | 4 | D | |

**Word Theme: WATER**

1) What the Romans built to transport water

2) Term for strong and fast-moving flood

3) Rise or fall of the sea that happens every day

4) Snake-like sea creature

5) A large body of water surrounded by land

6) The changing of a liquid into vapour

7) The military force that defends the seas

8) A sailing boat used for racing, or recreation

9) Reptile with a large shell that it uses for protection

10) Process of something being worn down by wind or water

11) Term referring to the sea, sailors or maritime subjects

12) Drink made using water, lemons and sugar

12

# Antonym Pairs 1

Difficulty Level: Easy

(Suggested completion time: 10 minutes)

> Select the two words, one from each group, that are the most **opposite** in meaning.
>
> .Example:        (cold  terrible  humid)      (speedy  horrible  fantastic)
>
> Answer: **terrible   fantastic**

1)                                      (unite  close  clean)   (spend  divide  thorough)

2)                                      (soft  plunge  separate)   (rise  shape  sculpt)

3)                                      (steep  sharp  scarce)   (relaxed  plentiful  wet)

4)                                      (flee  defend  flea)   (depart  remove  arrive)

5)                                      (frigid  valid  friendly)   (false  remote  cramped)

6)                                      (shoulder  ready  blame)   (raise  phrase  praise)

7)                                      (needy  neglect  fine)   (front  care  pass)

8)                                 (faded  careful  optimistic)   (cheerful  matted  gloomy)

9)                                 (eager  majestic  grudge)   (scent  disinterested  quilt)

10)                                 (peer  twilight  sincere)   (honest  honorary  deceitful)

11)                                 (cone  core  furnace)   (minor  major  main)

12)                                 (scatter  cry  freeze)   (pace  reach  assemble)

13)                                 (cold  necessary  fictional)   (non-essential  idle  gratitude)

14)                                 (embarrassed  fun  envy)   (confident  narrow  constrained)

15)                                 (towering  obvious  shabby)   (tardy  unclear  uninteresting)

# Antonym Pairs 2

Difficulty Level: Medium

(Suggested completion time: 10 minutes)

Select the two words, one from each group, that are the most **opposite** in meaning.

1)      (soil  grow  plant)     (decline  seed  flower)

2)      (dusty  smart  boastful)     (friendly  modest  chilly)

3)      (healthy  bandage  allergy)     (forward  sick  diagnosis)

4)      (defend  discourage  destroy)     (promote  neglect  withdraw)

5)      (generous  wealthy  courteous)     (affluent  miserly  efficient)

6)      (bright  bold  gigantic)     (timid  happy  fortunate)

7)      (prepared  popular  reluctant)     (fancy  bleak  keen)

8)      (steady  strict  swollen)     (lenient  stubborn  arrogant)

9)      (flowing  fasting  fleeting)     (crushing  splashing  enduring)

10)      (mystic  mayhem  matching)     (mood  calm  correct)

11)      (combined  orderly  adequate)     (smooth  solid  insufficient)

12)      (canny  danger  hammer)     (worker  safety  building)

13)      (typical  partial  cold)     (unusual  standard  sudden)

14)      (crowd  allow  post)     (ball  object  thing)

15)      (adjust  ascend  descend)     (feature  pull  drop)

# Antonym Pairs 3

Difficulty Level: Medium/Hard

(Suggested completion time: 10 minutes)

Select the two words, one from each group, that are the most **opposite** in meaning.

.

1)  (dusty  smart  skilful)  (clever  punctual  awkward)

2)  (engaged  obnoxious  impatient)  (delicious  believable  pleasant)

3)  (tender  guitar  cacophony)  (imitation  silence  harmony)

4)  (youthful  lethargic  spry)  (dangerous  elderly  juvenile)

5)  (ambivalent  artistic  ancient)  (conflicting  dated  modern)

6)  (weak  confined  complete)  (liberated  restricted  full)

7)  (deliberate  thoughtful  casual)  (connected  accidental  powerful)

8)  (author  novice  introvert)  (decency  trainee  expert)

9)  (utilise  compose  contradict)  (agree  confront  engage)

10)  (creative  natural  harmful)  (inadequate  serious  artificial)

11)  (detach  level  chip)  (shift  affix  support)

12)  (plausible  fearful  unkempt)  (grubby  tidy  remarkable)

13)  (shiny  vague  scientific)  (planetary  bright  distinct)

14)  (stationary  frequent  clear)  (obvious  angular  mobile)

15)  (touch  confuse  imagine)  (evade  clarify  compose)

# Antonym Pairs 4

Difficulty Level: Medium/Hard

(Suggested completion time: 10 minutes)

Select the word on the right that has the opposite meaning (is the best antonym) to the word in **bold** on the left.

*Example:* **smile**     laugh     shout     (frown)     grin     smirk

Answer:     **frown**

1) **blunt**          dull     pushy     tactful     sharp     gruff     short

2) **assist**          enable     assemble     discourage     incite     challenge

3) **constant**          steady     regular     stabile     variable     sneaky     compliant

4) **acknowledge**     absorb     information     undertake     deny     admit

5) **stubborn**          adamant     willful     creative     kind     flexible     shaky

6) **fatigue**          weariness     energy     uniform     camouflage     endless

7) **respectful**          civil     honest     gracious     hearty     impolite     studious

8) **destitute**          greedy     poor     bankrupt     affluent     careless

9) **feasible**          practical     viable     impossible     taxing     uncomplicated

10) **effortless**          facile     super     tragic     proficient     arduous     long

11) **sage**          unintelligent     sharp     arbitrary     stamina     wise     old

12) **vigilant**          straight     lightweight     careless     holy     prudent

13) **permit**          condone     classify     acquire     index     obstruct     license

14) **akin**          benefit     relaxed     unrelated     frustrated     abbreviated

15) **impeccable**     flawless     untouchable     caring     flawed     reliable

16

# Antonym Matching
Difficulty Level: Hard
(Suggested completion time: 10 minutes)

Match the word on the left with the word that has the opposite meaning on the right column.

| | |
|---|---|
| reluctant | discard |
| frivolous | tropical |
| retain | obey |
| conquer | honesty |
| spontaneous | practical |
| flourish | polite |
| ignore | enthusiastic |
| deception | careless |
| required | calculated |
| arctic | unnecessary |
| curt | lose |
| vigilant | wither |

# Synonym WORD BLOCKS 1

Difficulty Level: Easy/Medium
(Suggested completion time: 20 minutes)

Find a synonym for each of the given words, in the blocks of letters below. You may only use each letter in the block once. Letters must be connected, **including diagonally**, as shown in the example. The first letter of the answer has been highlighted and an arrow placed to the second. The total number of letters in the answer is also given.

*Example*: ALLOW
(6 letters)

| G | R | O |
|---|---|---|
| M | I | E |
| N | T | P |

*Answer*: PERMIT

1. ROBUST
(5 letters)

| A | G | F |
|---|---|---|
| N | D | S |
| O | R | T |

2. EXPAND
(5 letters)

| E | L | L |
|---|---|---|
| A | W | T |
| C | T | S |

3. INFERIOR
(6 letters)

| O | S | L |
|---|---|---|
| R | T | E |
| E | S | S |

4. ADEPT
(7 letters)

| C | O | E |
|---|---|---|
| A | B | L |
| P | A | M |

5. EMPTY
(6 letters)

| C | A | O |
|---|---|---|
| A | R | V |
| M | N | T |

6. BURDEN
(4 letters)

| D | A | Y |
|---|---|---|
| H | O | L |
| O | R | S |

7. SURPLUS
(6 letters)

| E | C | X |
|---|---|---|
| S | F | E |
| S | E | W |

8. SOLE
(4 letters)

| F | E | C |
|---|---|---|
| A | N | B |
| L | O | P |

18

**9. AGILE**
(6 letters)

| E | W | K |
|---|---|---|
| Q | L | C |
| U | G | B |
| N→ | I | M |

**10. ASSIGN**
(9 letters)

| T | E | U |
|---|---|---|
| A | R | G |
| N | D→ | E |
| G | I | S |

**11. AVOID**
(5 letters)

| S | O | P |
|---|---|---|
| T | D↓ | E |
| E | O | M |
| G | D | T |

**12. MEET**
(7 letters)

| C→ | O | N |
|---|---|---|
| A | T | T |
| E | G | A |
| R | T | C |

**13. FLOATS**
(7 letters)

| C | L | B |
|---|---|---|
| T | B→ | U |
| N | E | O |
| A | Y | G |

**14. ATTRACTIVE**
(6 letters)

| Y | H | E |
|---|---|---|
| A | T | P↓ |
| O | T | R |
| U | N | E |

**15. CAPTIVATING**
(8 letters)

| I | ←R | A |
|---|---|---|
| V | O | D |
| E | O | G |
| T | I | N |

**16. ABSURD**
(9 letters)

| H | L→ | U |
|---|---|---|
| S | A | D |
| U | E | I |
| O | R | C |

**17. HOME**
(7 letters)

| I | T | A |
|---|---|---|
| B | L | T |
| A | ←H | D |
| C | O | N |

**18. NEEDED**
(8 letters)

| Q | A | B |
|---|---|---|
| U | E↖ | U |
| I | R | R |
| D | E | N |

# Synonym WORD BLOCKS 2

## Difficulty Level: Medium/Hard
## (Suggested completion time: 10 minutes)

Find a synonym for each of the given words, in the blocks of letters below. You may only use each letter in the block once. Letters must be connected, **including diagonally**, as shown in the example. The first letter of the answer has been highlighted and an arrow placed to the second. The total number of letters in the answer is also given.

**1. CANCEL**
(7 letters)

| O | D | R |
|---|---|---|
| N | N | E |
| G | L | A |
| L | A→ | B |

**2. LUCRATIVE**
(10 letters)

| P→ | R | O |
|---|---|---|
| E | S | F |
| O | L | I |
| B | A | T |

**3. OBEDIENT**
(9 letters)

| I | L | P |
|---|---|---|
| A | Y | M |
| N | E | O↑ |
| T | A | C |

**4. DISTRESS**
(7 letters)

| R | O← | T |
|---|---|---|
| M | H | A |
| E | N | T |
| U | S | H |

**5. CHORTLE**
(5 letters)

| Y | R | C |
|---|---|---|
| H | O | L↓ |
| D | G | A |
| W | U | E |

**6. FATHOM**
(10 letters)

| D | C→ | O |
|---|---|---|
| N | L | M |
| E | S | P |
| H | E | R |

**7. ELUSIVE**
(8 letters)

| G | U | Y |
|---|---|---|
| P | E | R |
| A | P | C |
| S→ | L | I |

**8. SAFE**
(9 letters)

| D | I | A |
|---|---|---|
| E | S→ | H |
| R | O | E |
| E | T | L |

**9. VENERABLE**
(8 letters)

| E | E | L |
|---|---|---|
| T | R | M |
| S | E | A |
| E↑ | D | O |

**10. INTERFERE**
(7 letters)

| D | I | I |
|---|---|---|
| T | N↘ | A |
| R | I | Q |
| U | D | E |

# Synonym WORD BLOCKS 3

## Difficulty Level: Hard
### (Suggested completion time: 10 minutes)

Find an synonyms for each of the given words, in the blocks of letters below. You may only use each letter in the block once. Letters must be connected. For some the first letter of the answer has been highlighted. The total number of letters in the answer is also given.

**1. TEDIOUS** (6 letters)

| B | R | U |
|---|---|---|
| O | R | D |
| W | L | I |
| G | N | A |

**2. VIVACIOUS** (6 letters)

| A | Y | S |
|---|---|---|
| R | L | M |
| T | V | E |
| L | I | O |

**3. SURPASS** (6 letters)

| E | D | M |
|---|---|---|
| O | E | I |
| T | R | C |
| E | X | K |

**4. DISTORT** (5 letters)

| N | T | T |
|---|---|---|
| S | R | W |
| B | I | G |
| M | T | E |

**5. SOMBRE** (7 letters)

| I | R | A |
|---|---|---|
| O | E | V |
| U | S | O |
| L | S | J |

**6. NONCHALANT** (6 letters)

| K | L | N |
|---|---|---|
| E | A | O |
| U | H | T |
| S | A | C |

**7. ABHOR** (6 letters)

| S | P | M |
|---|---|---|
| I | D | E |
| T | S | T |
| A | W | E |

**8. JEOPARDY** (6 letters)

| F | U | N |
|---|---|---|
| R | A | G |
| D | E | S |
| O | R | T |

**9. BLUNDER** (7 letters)

| M | O | M |
|---|---|---|
| E | I | N |
| K | R | S |
| R | A | T |

**10. UNHURRIED** (4 letters)

| T | O | U |
|---|---|---|
| S | L | T |
| H | O | I |
| W | D | L |

# Antonym WORD BLOCKS 1

Difficulty Level: Easy/Medium
(Suggested completion time: 20 minutes)

Find an antonym for each of the given words, in the blocks of letters below. Connect the letters in the block going up or down, left or right. The letters must be <u>connected</u>. The first letter of the answer has been highlighted and an arrow placed toward the second. The total number of letters in the answer is also given.

*Example*: PLAIN
(5 letters)

*Answer*: FANCY

| T | R | F↓ |
|---|---|---|
| K | M | A |
| E | I | N |
| T | Y | C |

**1. DOUBT**
(5 letters)

| E | D | Q |
|---|---|---|
| T | I | P |
| S | O | R |
| U | R← | T |

**2. DISPUTE**
(5 letters)

| R | G← | A |
|---|---|---|
| E | A | T |
| E | I | S |
| P | N | D |

**3. DISMAL**
(6 letters)

| H | T | J |
|---|---|---|
| G | U | Y |
| I | B | K |
| R← | B | A |

**4. GENUINE**
(4 letters)

| B | W | C |
|---|---|---|
| M | F↓ | I |
| E | A | L |
| U | K | E |

**5. HAMPER**
(4 letters)

| E← | H | O |
|---|---|---|
| L | N | K |
| P | T | C |
| A | Y | L |

**6. RARE**
(6 letters)

| O | N | S |
|---|---|---|
| M | R | I |
| M | O← | C |
| P | L | E |

**7. GENTLE**
(6 letters)

| E | R | E |
|---|---|---|
| V | T | R |
| E↑ | U | I |
| S | S | M |

**8. FINISH**
(6 letters)

| F | O | Y |
|---|---|---|
| K | L | S |
| R | Q | E↓ |
| A | B | M |

## 9. DETACH (4 letters)

| N | I | O ↑ |
|---|---|---|
| S | H | **J** |
| C | R | I |
| M | O | V |

## 10. ENDLESS (7 letters)

| M | I | T |
|---|---|---|
| I ↑ | I | E |
| **L** | T | D |
| F | E | D |

## 11. CONTENT (7 letters)

| R | R | I |
|---|---|---|
| O ↑ | F | E |
| **W** | O | D |
| V | C | L |

## 12. DIMINISH (4 letters)

| R | L | P |
|---|---|---|
| O | R ← | **G** |
| W | F | T |
| C | L | O |

## 13. DIFFERENT (9 letters)

| **I** → | D | E |
|---|---|---|
| I | T | N |
| C | A | L |
| Q | P | M |

## 14. FRAGILE (6 letters)

| D | Y | H |
|---|---|---|
| R | E | E |
| U | T ← | **S** |
| R | F | K |

## 15. IGNORE (4 letters)

| S | B | A |
|---|---|---|
| O | I | D |
| R | M | E |
| G | **H** → | E |

## 16. AFFLUENT (4 letters)

| W | A | E |
|---|---|---|
| H | O ← | **P** |
| C | O | Y |
| I | R | H |

## 17. CORDIAL (7 letters)

| S | O ← | **H** |
|---|---|---|
| T | A | L |
| I | P | O |
| L | E | G |

## 18. YOUNG (7 letters)

| C | U | **E** ↓ |
|---|---|---|
| O | T | L |
| Y | H | D |
| L | R | E |

# Antonym WORD BLOCKS 2

## Difficulty Level: Medium/Hard
### (Suggested completion time: 10 minutes)

Find an antonyms for each of the given words, in the blocks of letters below. Connect the letters in the block going up or down, left or right. The letters must be <u>connected</u>. The first letter of the answer has been highlighted and an arrow placed to the second. The total number of letters in the answer is also given.

**1. FICKLE**
(8 letters)

| O | N | S |
|---|---|---|
| C | U | T |
| L | B | A |
| E | T | N |

**2. BROKEN**
(6 letters)

| O | L | T |
|---|---|---|
| H | E | C |
| T | R | A |
| I | N | T |

**3. HASTE**
(5 letters)

| E | D | F |
|---|---|---|
| L | S | A |
| A | T | N |
| Y | O | G |

**4. DORMANT**
(5 letters)

| R | A | L |
|---|---|---|
| E | W | A |
| E | P | K |
| T | S | E |

**5. STINGY**
(8 letters)

| U | S | O |
|---|---|---|
| O | C | R |
| R | O | G |
| E | N | E |

**6. NUISANCE**
(4 letters)

| F | R | I |
|---|---|---|
| L | E | H |
| P | U | O |
| A | D | N |

**7. VAGUE**
(5 letters)

| R | U | N |
|---|---|---|
| A | E | S |
| E | L | C |
| M | E | H |

**8. THWART**
(6 letters)

| T | S | I |
|---|---|---|
| O | A | S |
| R | O | S |
| N | I | A |

**9. ORDEAL**
(4 letters)

| A | O | S |
|---|---|---|
| H | N | I |
| C | A | L |
| B | L | M |

**10. ORIGIN**
(3 letters)

| N | E | C |
|---|---|---|
| D | L | O |
| L | A | P |
| H | P | Y |

# Antonym WORD BLOCKS 3

### Difficulty Level: Easy/Medium
### (Suggested completion time: 10 minutes)

Find an antonym for each of the given words, in the blocks of letters below. Connect the letters in the block going up or down, left or right. The letters must be <u>connected</u>. The first letter of the answer has been highlighted and an arrow placed to the second. The total number of letters in the answer is also given.

**1. ANCIENT**
(6 letters)

| A | R | O |
|---|---|---|
| C | E | C |
| N | R | E |
| A | T | N |

**2. GULLIBLE**
(10 letters)

| S | U | S |
|---|---|---|
| S | E | P |
| U | N | I |
| O | I | C |

**3. FAIR**
(6 letters)

| D | E | S |
|---|---|---|
| U | N | A |
| A | O | I |
| C | R | B |

**4. RUTHLESS**
(6 letters)

| G | E | N |
|---|---|---|
| H | O | T |
| I | F | L |
| A | D | E |

**5. UNITY**
(8 letters)

| V | I | D |
|---|---|---|
| I | A | I |
| S | W | R |
| I | O | N |

**6. SPEND**
(4 letters)

| O | M | S |
|---|---|---|
| E | V | A |
| U | I | N |
| R | E | A |

**7. CRAMPED**
(8 letters)

| U | S | E |
|---|---|---|
| O | O | C |
| I | R | S |
| C | A | P |

**8. PETITE**
(5 letters)

| F | O | S |
|---|---|---|
| E | M | M |
| G | R | A |
| T | L | L |

**9. SLOW**
(5 letters)

| L | R | W |
|---|---|---|
| S | A | E |
| A | P | C |
| F | I | D |

**10. APEX**
(6 letters)

| S | R | I |
|---|---|---|
| T | O | B |
| T | P | E |
| O | M | D |

25

# CROSSWORD 1 (ANTONYMS )

Difficulty Level: Medium (with Word Bank)
(Suggested completion time: 30 minutes)

The clue is the **opposite** of the word needed. Use the word bank to help.

## Across:

3) Proceed

6) This won't last

7) Repeatedly

10) Let's get it together!

12) It's compulsory

15) Lead

18) Selected with care

21) Depart

22) Secretive

23) Bold

24) Inferior grade

## Down:

1) Worst

2) Balloon!

3) Let's fix this

4) Snow upon snow

5) What a cacophony!

8) Unprepared

9) Now this is important

11) Question this

13) Head

14) Smooth

16) In favour of

17) That's rude

18) Oh dear, that's bad!

19) Include

20) Obey

## WORD BANK – ACROSS

| | |
|---|---|
| COY | WAIT |
| RANDOM | QUALITY |
| SCATTER | ONCE |
| VOLUNTARY | SURVIVE |
| OVERT | LAG |
| REMAIN | |

## WORD BANK – DOWN

| | |
|---|---|
| COURTEOUS | DEFY |
| AGAINST | REJOICE |
| OMIT | SHRINK |
| BEST | ROUGH |
| TRIVIAL | SOLUTION |
| WRECK | READY |
| TAIL | SILENCE |
| THAW | |

# CROSSWORD 2 (ANTONYMS)

Difficulty Level: Medium (With Word Bank)
(Suggested completion time: 30 minutes)

The clue is the **opposite** of the word needed. Use the Word Bank to help.

## Across:
1) Release
4) Humid
6) Freezes
7) Feeble
9) Later on
10) Unexceptional
12) Provide
13) Trust
14) Pro (for)
16) Bravery
19) Affirmative
21) Straight
22) Confirm
23) Transparent
24) Boring, Dull
27) Release
29) Improve
30) Modesty
31) Begin
32) Desert
33) Rejoice
34) Extinguish
35) Optimist

## Down:
1) Urge
2) Care for, give attention to
3) Consonant
4) Timid
5) Silence
8) Something new
11) Unite
15) Remain the same
16) Shows, reveals
17) Repel
18) Strict
20) Narrow
25) Hide
26) Horizontal
27) Conceal, suppress
28) Honesty
30) Underwhelming

## WORD BANK – ACROSS

| | |
|---|---|
| CEASE | COWARDICE |
| STRONG | TENSE |
| CATCH | IGNITE |
| DETAIN | SOON |
| BENT | OPAQUE |
| ANTI | PECULIAR |
| CYNIC | BOILS |
| EGO | NAY |
| DECEIT | SEA |
| ARID | GRIEVE |
| ROT | TAKE |
| REJECT | |

## WORD BANK – DOWN

| | |
|---|---|
| HOAX | ASSERTIVE |
| ERECT | CONVEY |
| EPIC | BROAD |
| LENIENT | ATTRACT |
| TRANSFORM | NEGLECT |
| VOWEL | DIN |
| EMERGE | RELIC |
| DISSUADE | CONCEALS |
| SEPARATE | |

# CROSSWORD 3

Difficulty Level: Medium
(Suggested completion time: 30 minutes)

Use the clues to find the right answer in the crossword puzzle

## Across

1) Never a show-off

3) Playful mocking, but it can hurt

8) A small hill

9) Describing things that are nearby

10) A failure

11) Destroy forever

13) A heavenly creature

14) This happens often

18) A small amount

19) The same as

20) Sometimes snatched from the jaws of defeat

22) Cunning, crafty

23) Demise

25) How very strange

27) Squirrels and mice are these

29) What horses say

30) What is usual, standard

## Down

1) Stop!

2) Get bigger

3) Storm

4) An angle of less than 90°

5) Put up with something

6) Belt clasp

7) Complicated

10) Absolutely perfect

12) This is far more than necessary

13) Having no hair on the head

15) Wild, not domesticated

16) A type of sailboat

17) A defence used in court

21) This poetry is confusing

24) Arrange things straight or parallel

26) To worry unnecessarily

28) To go downwards

29) Grab

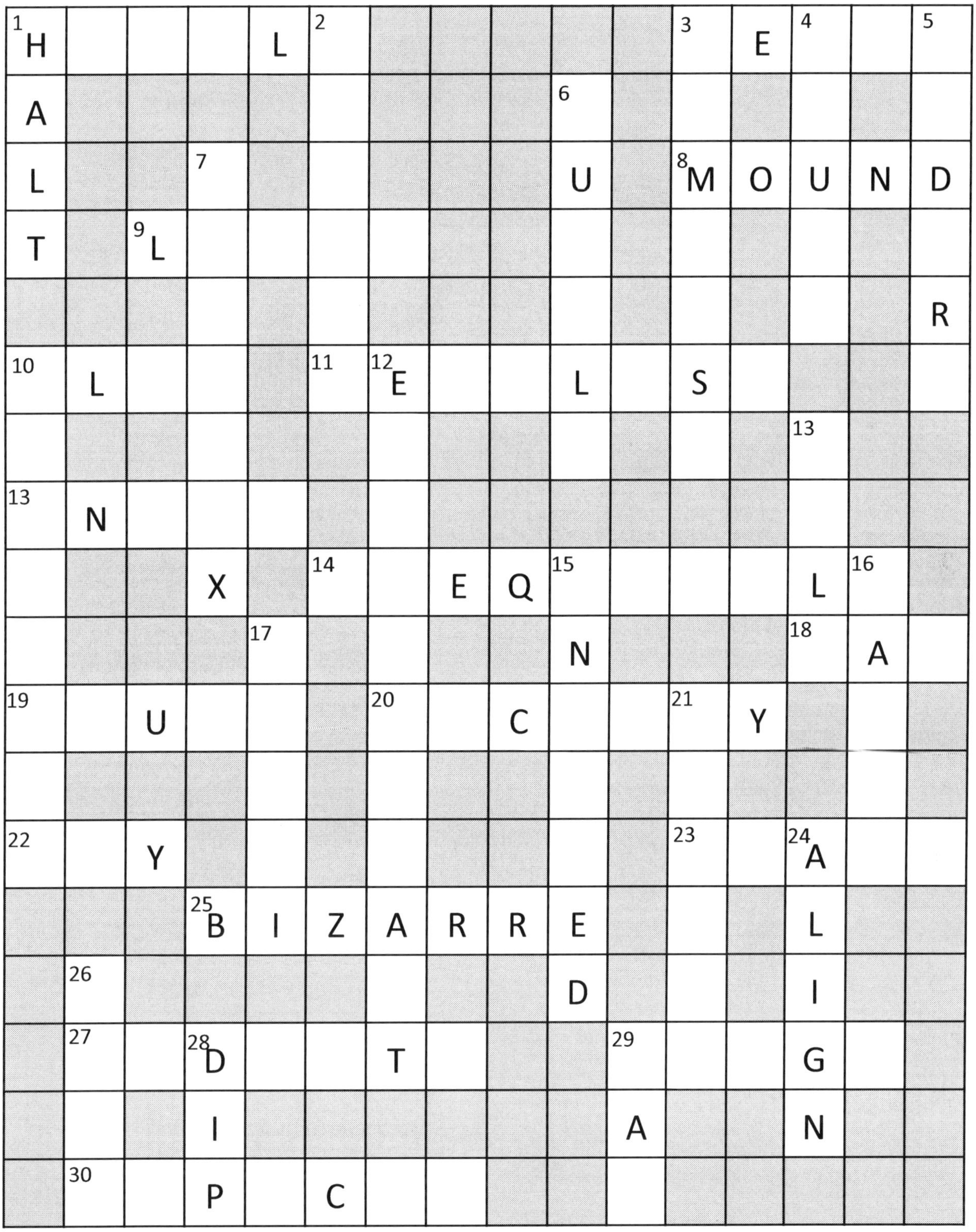
MOUND
BIZARRE

# CROSSWORD 4

Difficulty Level: Medium
(Suggested completion time: 30 minutes)

Use the clues to find the right answer in the crossword puzzle

## Across

3) STOP!

6) Diminish

7) What a catastrophe!

10) On time

11) Volvo and Audi are examples

12) Ghastly and horrid

15) To perish

16) That's not very clear

17) To challenge, resist

23) Very worried

24) A booking or performance by musicians

25) Strong and healthy

26) Told a fabrication

27) Nobody here

## Down

1) A victory

2) A model often made from stone, clay or wood

4) Your mother's sister

5) Terminate

7) To be in agreement

8) How lazy

9) Rough, opposite of soft

11) To give up, or surrender control

13) A male deer

14) An assistant

18) Bendy

19) Having a pleasant smell

20) A type of top worn by women

21) Treat an infection with this amount of medicine

22) A list of things to be done

23) The month before May

Crossword grid (page 33). Cell contents with clue numbers and filled letters:

| C1 | C2 | C3 | C4 | C5 | C6 | C7 | C8 | C9 | C10 | C11 |
|----|----|----|----|----|----|----|----|----|----|----|
| ¹T |  |  |  | 2 |  | 3 | E | 4 | S | 5 |
| ⁶ | E | D |  |  | E |  |  |  |  |  |
| I |  |  |  |  |  |  |  |  |  | D |
|  |  | ⁷C |  |  |  |  | ⁸I |  | Y |  |
|  |  | O |  | P |  |  |  |  |  | ⁹C |
| ¹⁰ |  | N |  |  |  | A |  |  |  | O |
| H |  | C |  |  |  |  | E |  |  |  |
|  |  | U |  | R |  |  |  | ¹¹C |  |  |
|  | ¹² | R |  |  | ¹³ |  |  | E |  |  |
| ¹⁴A |  |  |  |  | T |  |  | ¹⁵D |  |  |
| I |  |  |  | ¹⁶ |  | G |  | E |  |  |
| ¹⁷D |  | ¹⁸ | Y |  |  |  |  |  |  | ¹⁹ |
| E |  | L |  | ²⁰ |  | ²¹ |  |  |  | R |
|  |  |  |  |  |  |  |  | ²² |  |  |
| ²³A | N | X | I | O | U | S |  | ²⁴G | I | G |
|  |  |  |  |  |  |  |  |  |  |  |
| ²⁵ | O |  |  | S |  |  |  |  |  |  |
|  |  |  |  |  |  |  |  | D |  | N |
| ²⁶ |  |  | D |  | ²⁷ |  | C |  |  | T |

# CROSSWORD 5

Difficulty Level: Medium
(Suggested completion time: 30 minutes)

Use the clues to find the right answer in the crossword puzzle

Across:

1) Oh dear, that's a bad sign.

3) That was difficult, and the spelling too

6) An engine or horse may pull this

8) A cartographer would make this

9) Concealed

11) Run quickly

12) A place of worship

15) A very smart aquatic mammal

16) How extraordinary!

17) Comfortable

18) Someone who is adored

20) Glad to get here

22) Wonder, amazement

24) And so on (abbreviation)

25) Artists use this to display a picture

26) The opposite of pollute

Down:

1) Let the music play here

2) The 3rd planet from the sun

4) The opposite of love

5) Fowl

7) The winner's medal

10) Necessary, truly needed

13) Oh dear! It cost a lot

14) A house with just one floor

15) All wrong

17) You might find baby here

19) Leave out

21) A covering, often worn by a bride

23) Not complicated

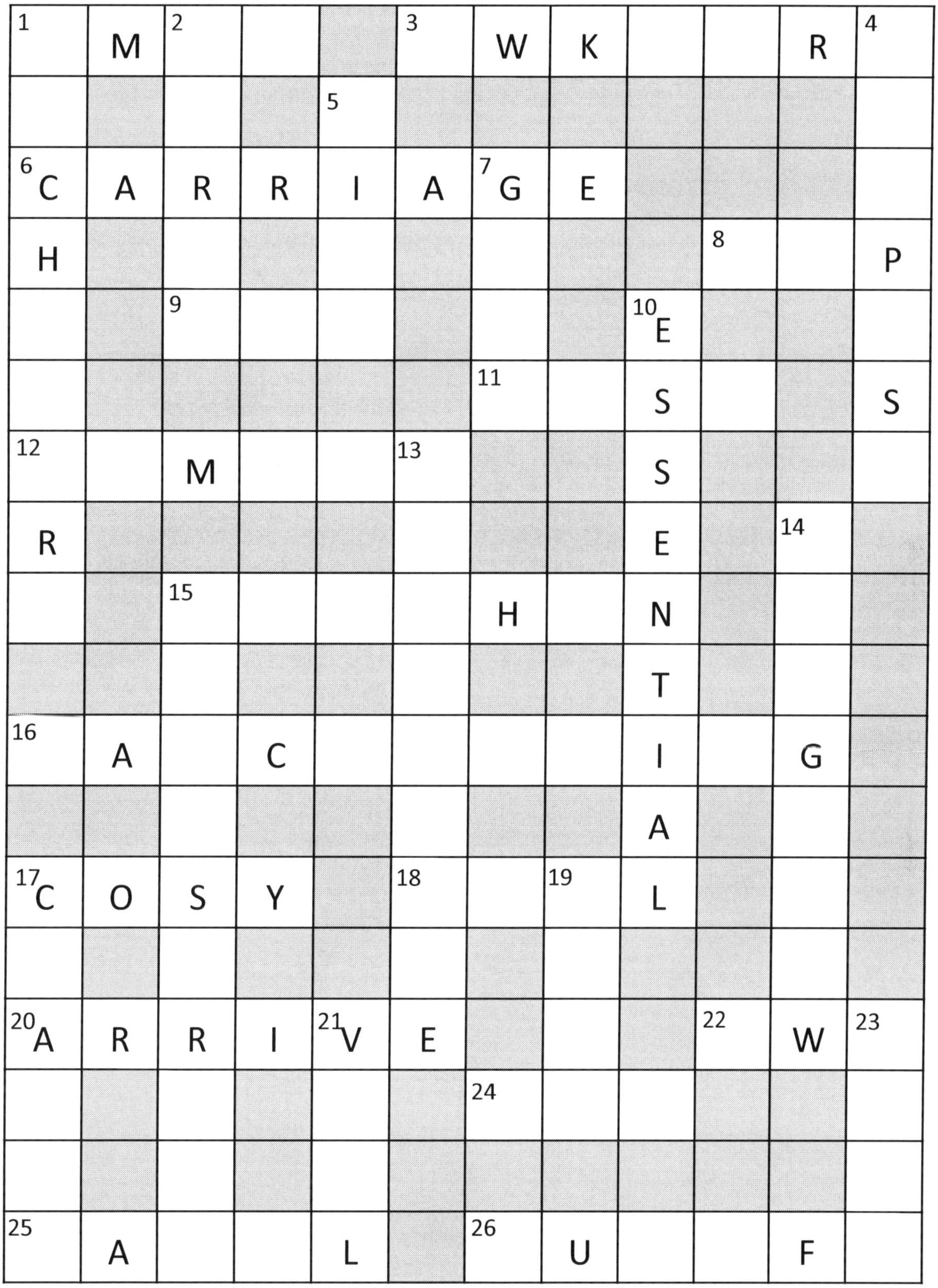

Crossword grid (12 columns):

| | | | | | | | | | | | |
|---|---|---|---|---|---|---|---|---|---|---|---|
| [1] | M | [2] | | | [3] | W | K | | | R | [4] |
| | | | | [5] | | | | | | | |
| [6]C | A | R | R | I | A | [7]G | E | | | | |
| H | | | | | | | | | [8] | | P |
| | | [9] | | | | | [10]E | | | | S |
| | | | | | [11] | | S | | | | S |
| [12] | | M | | [13] | | | S | | [14] | | |
| R | | | | | | | E | | | | |
| | | [15] | | | | H | N | | | | |
| | | | | | | | T | | | | |
| [16] | A | | C | | | | I | | G | | |
| | | | | | | | A | | | | |
| [17]C | O | S | Y | | [18] | | [19] | L | | | |
| | | | | | | | | | | | |
| [20]A | R | R | I | [21]V | E | | | | [22] | W | [23] |
| | | | | | [24] | | | | | | |
| [25] | A | | | L | | [26] | U | | | F | |

# CROSSWORD 6

Difficulty Level: Hard
(Suggested completion time: 30 minutes)

Use the clues to find the right answer in the crossword puzzle

<u>Across:</u>

1) Achieve

2) Homonym of peace

5) Attach or fasten

7) Up we go

9) Keep moving

10) Describing rapid movement

11) The act of a show-off

12) That's fancy and expensive

14) Small bag for carrying money

16) Timid

18) A hermit

20) They decide

21) A house with ghosts

23) Well, that's rude!

<u>Down:</u>

1) The way in

2) It's only going to get worse!

3) The 5<sup>th</sup> prime number

4) Looking back

6) The 11+, for example

8) Genre of film or theatre

10) A banquet

11) Fights with gloves on

13) Alter

14) Could do with some water

15) Place where hairdressers work

17) Small island

19) Shows you the way

22) Also

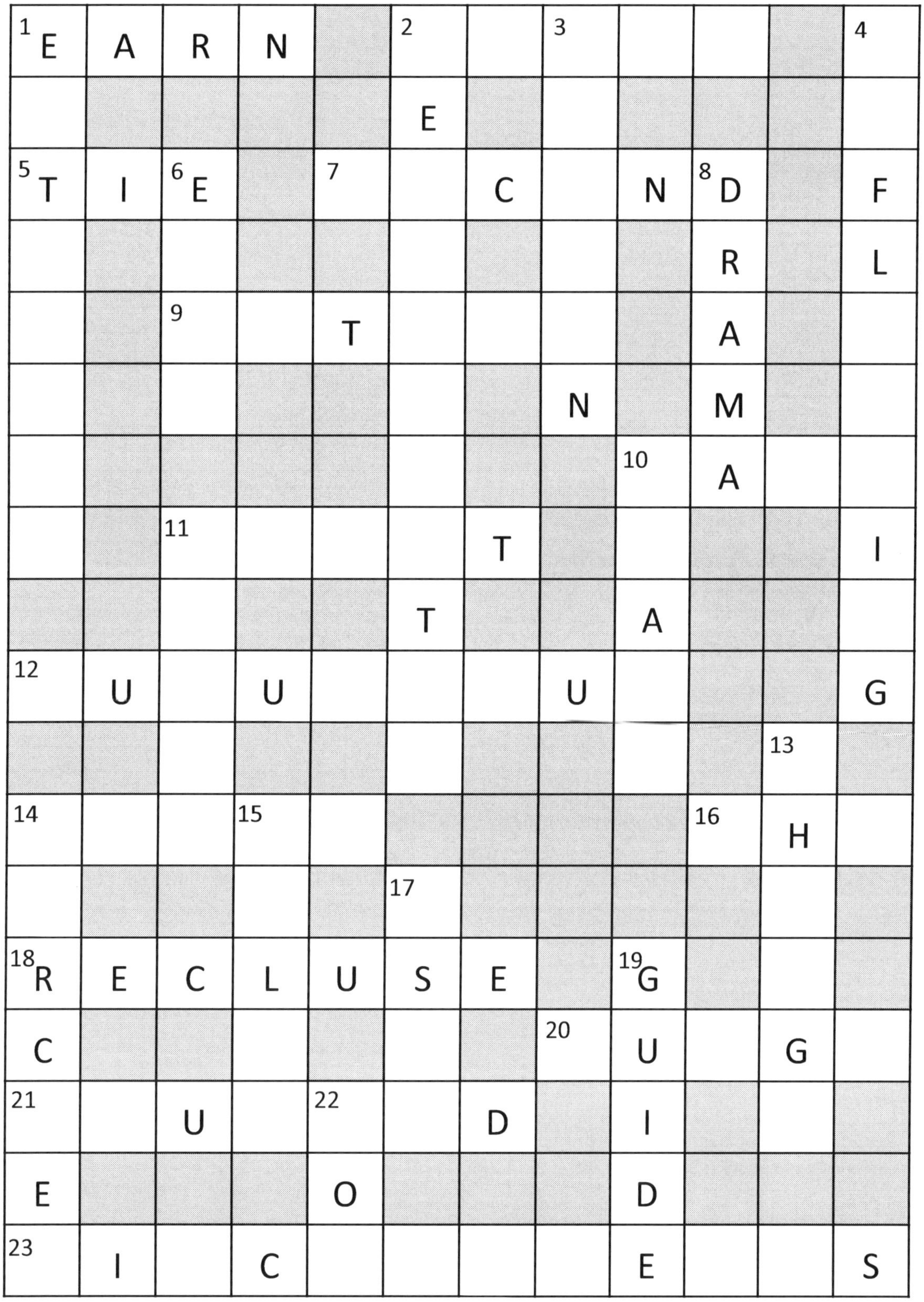

# CROSSWORD 7

Difficulty Level: Hard
(Suggested completion time: 30 minutes)

Use the clues to find the right answer in the crossword puzzle

<u>Across:</u>

1) Well behaved

4) Here to help

7) Bovines

8) Top part of a house

9) Discipline for bad behaviour

10) Very simple

13) Northeast (abbreviation)

14) Run at a moderate pace

15) Stationary

16) Push gently

17) Despicable

20) Fashionable

22) Uncooked

24) Less than the whole

25) Showing extreme anger

26) Dark, dim

29) Impedes, slows down

31) That's annoying!

<u>Down:</u>

1) A job I do regularly for money

2) This is getting longer

3) Large African or Asian mammal

5) It's not easy

6) You may find this in a hot cross bun

11) Taking of something by force

12) Easily broken

15) Plants seeds

18) Right away (abbreviation)

19) It's pretty cold

20) Not bending or curving

21) Term for umbrella

23) Frail

27) Feel sadness over a loss

28) A scheme

30) Gave it a rest

# CROSSWORD 8

Difficulty Level: Hard
(Suggested completion time: 30 minutes)

Use the clues to find the right answer in the crossword puzzle

## Across:

1) This is very, very hot

6) Form of precipitation

7) You can see this

8) Browse the Internet

9) Nitrogen and oxygen are examples

10) Cry like a baby

13) At a great distance

15) By mouth or voice

16) A large cloud of smoke

18) Fled

19) Talk about secrets, some of which are not true

21) A big hug

24) Divisible by two

26) Utilise

29) No bumps here

31) Something that needs to be done

32) Prohibit

36) Copy or imitate

37) Make lighter (in colour)

38) Keen

40) Not even

41) Doesn't sound good, but can be average

42) Feeling famished

## Down:

1) Wild

2) Nice to find in the desert

3) Empty inside

4) Hold on to tightly

5) All the same

11) Structure where sporting or entertainment events take place

12) A small dwelling

13) An extremely quick moment in time

14) Reduce use

16) The here and now

17) Cause harm

20) Grows in a pod

22) A tiny piece

23) Radiant light used in signs

25) Not difficult

27) Fly upward

28) Wide gap or deep opening

30) Rotten to the core

33) Totally isolated

34) Sharp claw on an eagle

35) Building used for storage

36) Large cup with a handle

39) An extremely long time ago

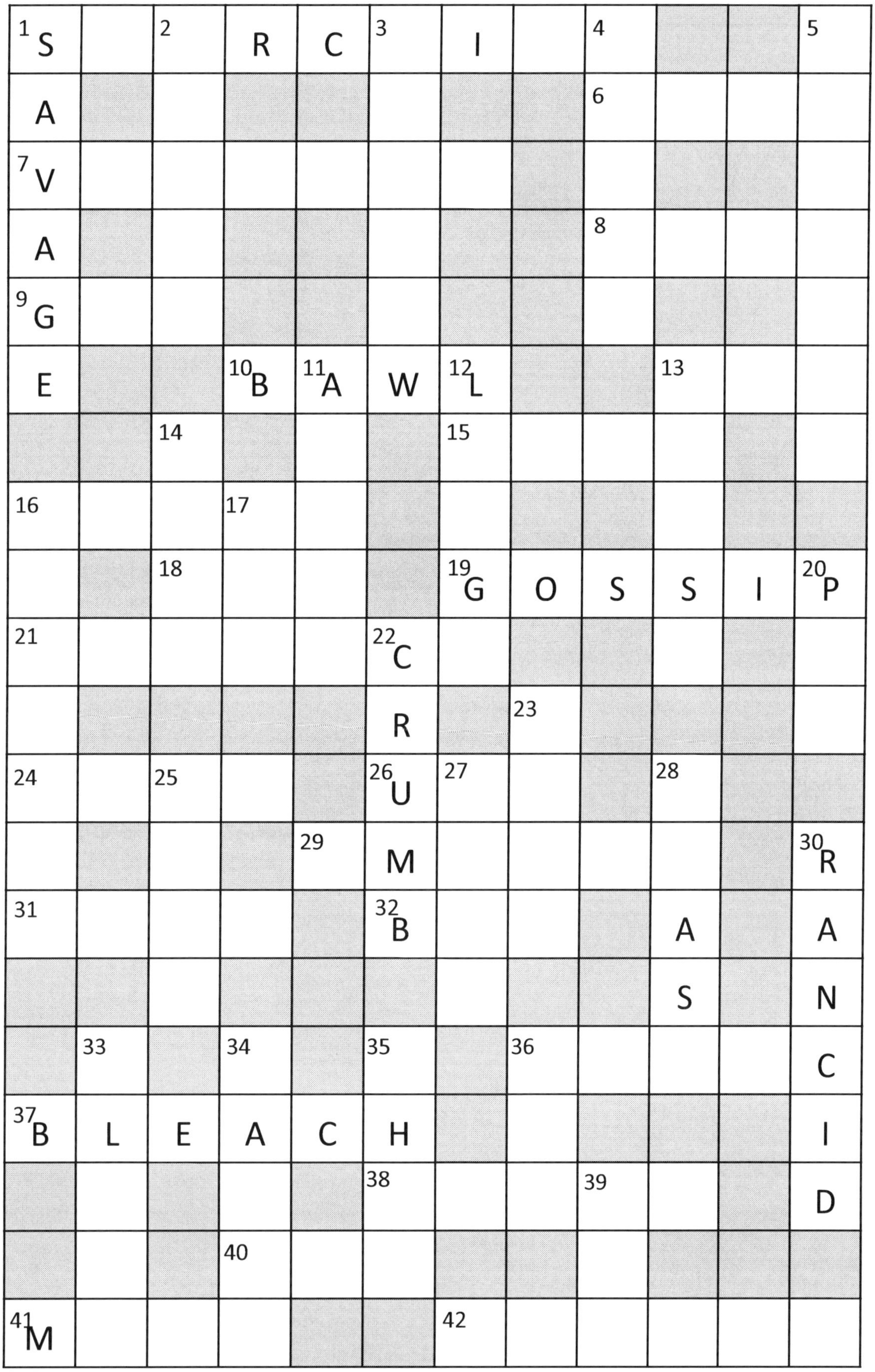

Crossword grid (page 41)

Row 1: [1] S · [2] · R · C · [3] I · · [4] · · [5]
Row 2: A · · · · · · [6]
Row 3: [7] V · · · · · ·
Row 4: A · · · · · [8]
Row 5: [9] G · · · · · · ·
Row 6: E · · [10] B · [11] A · W · [12] L · · [13]
Row 7: · · [14] · · · [15]
Row 8: [16] · · [17]
Row 9: · · [18] · · · [19] G · O · S · S · I · [20] P
Row 10: [21] · · [22] C
Row 11: · · · R · · [23]
Row 12: [24] · [25] · · [26] U · [27] · · [28]
Row 13: · · · [29] · M · · · [30] R
Row 14: [31] · · · · [32] B · · · A · · A
Row 15: · · · · · · · S · N
Row 16: · [33] · [34] · [35] · [36] · · · C
Row 17: [37] B · L · E · A · C · H · · · I
Row 18: · · · · [38] · · [39] · · D
Row 19: · · [40]
Row 20: [41] M · · · · [42]

# JUST FOR PUN

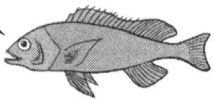

42

Why was the calendar depressed?

Because its days were numbered.

I fell asleep last night still wearing my glasses.

My dreams have never been clearer.

§

My mum never seems to have any herbs.

She's always telling me she's out of thyme.

§

What maths aid is the most supportive of farming?

The protractor

§

What did the mirror say after it lost the contest?

'I need some time to reflect.'

Why did the football stadium get so hot at the end of the match?

All the fans left.

§

You don't like fantasy stories?

No, they tend to dragon.

§

When I complained that it was too cold in the house, my brother told me to stand in the corner – it was 90°

My father used to work at an upholstery shop. He's fully recovered now.

§

Someone added more dirt to my garden!

The plot thickens.

§

The fisherman could never catch anything so he gave up and went to work for a dolphin.. It doesn't pay well, but at least he serves a porpoise.

# Anagrams 1
Difficulty Level: Easy
(Suggested completion time: 5 minutes)

In these sentences, there is a word that has the letters jumbled. Select the word below that is the correct version of the jumbled word.

*Example:*

Matt **GINSED** up for a class to learn how to make pottery.

a. DEIGNS    b. DESIGN    c. SINGED    d. SIGNED

1) The vegetation in the tundra was **PARESS**.

   a. SPARES    b. SPARSE    c. SPEARS    d. PARSES

2) If symptoms **SPRIEST** for more than three days, then see a doctor.

   a. SPRITES    b. ESPRITS    c. STRIPES    d. PERSIST

3) Nate found the **DEARTHS** part of the project was getting started.

   a. HARDEST    b. THREADS    c. HATREDS    d. TRASHED

4) The policeman was **DELTAER** to a possible crime in progress.

   a. ALTERED    b. RELATED    c. TREADLE    d. ALERTED

5) Lottie went **YAELR** to the store to make sure they had bread.

   a. LAYER    b. RELAY    c. EARLY    d. LEARY

6) Mum knew there was too much at **TEAKS** to be distracted by such a small matter.

   a. TAKES    b. STEAK    c. SKATE    d. STAKE

7) Dad used to say that it always looks **RESOW** than it actually is.

   a. OWERS    b. WORSE    c. SWORE    d. SOWER

8) Greg's numerous **LAPSE** for extra time on the assignment were ignored.

   a. PALES    b. LEAPS    c. PLEAS    d. PEALS

9) There was a **RAWDER** for finding the lost kitten.

   a. REWARD    b. DRAWER    c. REDRAW    d. WARRED

10) Within the **NASP** of an hour, Dora managed to complete all of her homework.

   a. SPAP    b. PANS    c. SPAN    d. SNAP

# Anagrams 2
Difficulty Level: Medium/Hard
(Suggested completion time: 10 minutes)

Rearrange the letters of the jumbled word on the left and write it in the blank at the right. Use the hint to help.

*Example:*

| | | |
|---|---|---|
| CLAUCIR | It's absolutely necessary | CRUCIAL |
| | | *Answer* |

1)  LDMISA          Not just bad, but extremely bad          _____

2)  RAMON          A large, grand home          _____

3)  LEBLSMHEI          Make something sound better than it is          _____

4)  TUURRPE          Causing something to tear or split          _____

5)  CINGOINOT          Going in disguise          _____

6)  QESAUL          Make a high-pitched noise          _____

7)  VOICEN          A beginner          _____

8)  BALETT          A pill, or type of computer          _____

9)  DIVIL          Angry or irate          _____

10)  DRIFIG          Very cold          _____

11)  RECARIT          Unpredictable          _____

12)  YUGMG          very warm and humid          _____

45

# Anagrams 3

Difficulty Level: Hard
(Suggested completion time: 15 minutes)

Rearrange the letters of the jumbled word on the left and write it in the blank at the right. Use the hint to help.

1) MONILAN       Something minimal or insignificant       _____

2) RAVEGEA       Mediocre       _____

3) ELMDED       Interfere without permission       _____

4) LENSUL       Bad-tempered       _____

5) MIORPATNT       Of great significance       _____

6) TRUST       Walk confidently       _____

7) PVECEIDTE       Misleading       _____

8) SELUDNIO       A mistaken belief       _____

9) SAMRENNT       Small pieces left over from a larger item       _____

10) SCOPE       A small group of trees       _____

11) DUTERRPBE       Feeling bothered or worried       _____

12) NEEGUIN       Authentic       _____

13) VAIWE       Give up, or abandon       _____

14) QUENSDAR       Lose through being careless       _____

15) SOULUBEN       Hazy, vague, unclear       _____

# Anagrams 4

Difficulty Level: Medium/Hard

(Suggested completion time: 10 minutes)

Look at the word on the left. By rearranging the letters, you should be able to form different words on the right. Some have more than one answer.

*Example:*

CAR

| A | R | C |
|---|---|---|

1) MALE

2) READ

3) TEAM

4) POLO

5) BREAK

6) CHARM

7) ROUTE

8) LUMBER

9) AMUSES

10) LISTEN

# JUST FOR FUN

## Word Scramble

Find the answer to each of questions by looking at the picture clue and filling in the missing letters. Then answer the last question by using all the letters in the boxes.

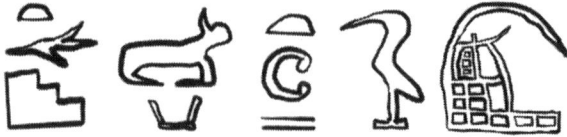

H I ☐ R O ☐ L Y __ H

__ ☐ R __ M I D

S ☐ ☐ R A B

(beetle)

__ P H ☐ ☐ X

☐ H A __ A O __

What is the main theme of these words?

| | N | | E | T | | | | | T |
|---|---|---|---|---|---|---|---|---|---|

# Compound Words 1
## Difficulty Level: Easy
### (Suggested completion time: 8 minutes)

In these exercises, pick the word from the choices given, that will together with the bold word form a new compound word.

*Example:*

**hand**    A. tail   B. miss   C. grow   D. shake   E. tube        __**D. handshake**__
                                                                                    *Answer*

1) **water**   A. ocean   B. rough   C. fall   D. wrap   E. rattle   _____

2) **table**   A. chain   B. relax   C. fork   D. spoon   E. knife   _____

3) **bar**   A. slim   B. gain   C. train   D. growth   E. win   _____

4) **rain**   A. earth   B. circular   C. bow   D. planet   E. farm   _____

5) **under**   A. thin   B. care   C. full   D. extra   E. estimate   _____

6) **friend**   A. ship   B. through   C. dock   D. anchor   _____

7) **board**   A. ceiling   B. sprint   C. walk   D. crawl   E. hit   _____

8) **rocket**   A. missile   B. ship   C. craft   D. cushion   E. arc   _____

9) **head**   A. torso   B. sole   C. brick   D. circle   E. band   _____

10) **finger**   A. steal   B. branch   C. hair   D. nail   E. palm   _____

11) **cart**   A. cabin   B. computer   C. roof   D. wheel   E. tyre   _____

12) **blue**   A. turquoise   B. shady   C. berry   D. opal   E. feel   _____

# Compound Words 2
Difficulty Level: Medium
(Suggested completion time: 8 minutes)

In these exercises, pick two words, one from each group in brackets, that will together form a new closed compound word – <u>with the correct spelling.</u> Fill in the word in the blank.

*Example:* (hair  blonde  fashion)  (mist  spray  wig)        **hairspray**
                                                                                                       *Answer*

1)   (rain  flame  aero)  (helicopter  stretcher  plane)        _____

2)   (arm  leg  finger)  (lip  recliner  chair  lounge)        _____

3)   (miss  tooth  brain)  (take  cream  paste)        _____

4)   (dolphin  cat  horse)  (probe  play  flipper)        _____

5)   (blaze  cinder  candle)  (hearth  coal  light)        _____

6)   (body  form  coffer)  (protect  guard  locker)        _____

7)   (story  book  volume)  (store  library  basket)        _____

8)   (elbow  shoulder  hand)  (shove  hit  shake)        _____

9)   (news  media  internet)  (screen  paper  relay)        _____

10)  (head  main  capital)  (stream  river  sea)        _____

11)  (peak  high  centre)  (streak  glow  light)        _____

12)  (sock  trousers  shoe)  (flare  lace  trace)        _____

# Compound Words 3

In these exercises, pick two words, one from each group in brackets, that will together form a new closed compound word – <u>with the correct spelling.</u> Fill in the word in the blank.

1) (contract note chord) (worthy ring blank) _____

2) (mental brain thought) (clean wash wipe) _____

3) (proof print detail pen) (scan read phone chat) _____

4) (eve day twilight night) (crack fall slide taxi) _____

5) (epoch era time minute) (series course line) _____

6) (extra under wheel) (land typical ordinary) _____

7) (false wrong bring take) (being maker doing) _____

8) (early plain common) (money coins wealth) _____

9) (fort wall brick stone) (night evening castle) _____

10) (home stay here up) (noon after there) _____

11) (sit crawl stand lay) (free through over under) _____

12) (torso tail tense tall) (bane bail ball bone) _____

# Spreading the Word – 1

> In this exercise, you will be given a clue, and then must find the hidden word that is spread out between the <u>end</u> of the first word and <u>beginning</u> of the second.
>
> *Examples:*
>
> | Physical or mental suffering | conduc<u>tor</u>  <u>ment</u>ality | (answer: torment) |
> | Get larger | refl<u>ex</u>  <u>pand</u>a | (answer: expand) |

1) Bring up a child as one's own; take on          nomad    optician

2) Not friendly or involved, distant          halo    official

3) Be made up of          beacon    sister

4) Happen          havoc    curiosity

5) Desolate, dreary          amiable    akin

6) Confident and fast-talking, but not sincere          bowling    liberty

7) Deadly          sofa    talisman

8) Temporarily stop something          consensus    pendulum

9) Contain or limit use of something          occur    balloon

10) Wise, clever          visa    genuine

# S p r e a d i n g   t h e   W o r d – 2
## Difficulty Level: Medium
### (Suggested completion time: 10 minutes)

In this exercise, you will be given a clue, and then must find the hidden word that is spread out between the <u>end</u> of the first word and <u>beginning</u> of the second.

1) Someone who helps and provides support      rudimental    lyrical

2) Not tidy, uncared for      chipmunk    emptiness

3) Obstruct, impede      dolphin    derelict

4) Speech, usually on a religious subject      hairdresser    monumental

5) Dedicate all your time and effort      countryside    voters

6) Expression of grief or sorrow      bedlam    entertain

7) Diminish or put concerns at rest      subliminal    layover

8) Pay attention or take note of      breathe    edible

9) Somewhat indecent, rude      debris    quenched

10) Peaceful, calm      composer    energise

11) Relating to the moon      flu    narrative

12) Conceited      balaclava    inevitable

# Spreading the Word – 3

Difficulty Level: Medium
(Suggested completion time: 10 minutes)

In this exercise, you will be given a clue, and then must find the hidden word that is spread out between the <u>end</u> of the first word and <u>beginning</u> of the second.

1) Unruly, loud                                  arrow    dynamic

2) Legally responsible                           memorabilia    bleach

3) Gently persuade                               calico    axis

4) Scoundrel, unprincipled person               superhero    guest

5) Only, just                                    extreme    resemble

6) Express regret for one's actions             meagre    penthouse

7) Stay somewhere longer than necessary         penicillin    germane

8) A smell                                       livelihood    ourselves

9) Someone who betrays a person or cause        portrait    orator

10) Occupant                                     forgotten    antibacterial

11) Force to do                                  intercom    pelican

12) Extreme danger                               zookeeper    illuminating

# JUST FOR FUN
## Cloze Word Search
### HOLIDAYS

Find the words in the puzzle from the clues below. All of the words will relate to holidays.

1) Spending the night in a tent or caravan    C ☐ ☐ P I ☐ G

2) Help you see better in the bright sun    ☐ U ☐ G L ☐ ☐ S ☐ S

3) What you need to go to a different country    P A ☐ ☐ P O ☐ T

4) You might need this to prevent sunburns    S ☐ N S ☐ R ☐ ☐ N

5) Used to carry items when you go hiking    B ☐ ☐ K ☐ A ☐ K

6) Where you might go swimming    ☐ I ☐ O

7) Where you might stay in a city    H ☐ T ☐ L

8) Used to put clothing in for a big trip    ☐ U ☐ G ☐ ☐ E

9) Old-fashioned way to send a picture by mail    P ☐ S ☐ C A ☐ D

10) A person who visits an area for pleasure    T O ☐ R ☐ S ☐

```
B  U  S  I  D  R  A  C  T  S  O  P  B
A  K  M  U  Y  N  I  P  A  S  S  C  A
R  C  S  U  N  S  C  R  E  E  N  L  C
M  A  P  A  K  G  N  I  P  M  A  C  K
C  P  C  R  T  E  L  A  E  L  T  E  L
A  K  G  O  E  G  S  A  R  D  O  T  H
R  C  U  P  A  S  S  E  S  G  L  O  S
D  A  D  E  P  T  A  L  G  S  T  I  W
E  B  T  O  U  R  I  S  T  E  E  J  P
G  O  R  A  S  O  D  I  L  A  O  S  Q
A  T  I  H  L  U  G  G  A  G  E  B  L
```

# Connections 1
Difficulty Level: Medium
(Suggested completion time: 8 minutes)

Select the word from the group of words in the middle of the page, that has a similar meaning to the words listed in each of the brackets on the right and left sides.

Example: (volume, tome)    copy (book) scroll / manual    (schedule, organise)

Example: (section, chunk)    stop / clog / wall (block)    (hinder, thwart)

1) (orderly, constant)    akin / consistent / suit / uniform / habit    (attire, costume)

2) (devour, gobble)    pack / gorge / fissure / guzzle / gulch    (chasm, ravine)

3) (now, today)    present / furnish / current / start / commence    (award, donate)

4) (club, gang)    outfit/ party / belt / band / bond / society    (ring, chain)

5) (pot, container)    dish / bowl / basin / throw / cup    (pitch, hurl)

6) (dazzling, luminous)    smart / glitter / radiant / bright    (clever, intelligent)

7) (healthy, fit)    strong / well / source / fountain / fresh    (reservoir, basin)

8) (deceive, con)    distort / lie / mislead / laze / recline    (rest, sprawl)

9) (husk, covering)    snap / case / blanket / shell / bark    (howl, yelp)

10) (comfort, soothe)    relieve / remote / console / duplex    (dashboard, panel)

# Connections 2
Difficulty Level: Medium
(Suggested completion time: 8 minutes)

Select the word from the group of words in the middle of the page, that has a similar meaning to the words listed in each of the brackets on the right and left sides.

1) (modern, contemporary)    present / circular / current / run / ebb    (flow, stream)

2) (dispute, oppose)    contest / debate / controversy / sport    (competition, game)

3) (jump, leap)    hop / vault / spring / coil / geyser / fountain    (water source)

4) (trend, fashion)    fad / mode / convention / method / vein    (manner, way)

5) (conspiracy, plot)    maneuver / ruse / pique / intrigue / charm    (attract, fascinate)

6) (amusing, humorous)    whimsical / curious / funny / bizarre    (weird, strange)

7) (company, business)    compact / firm / enterprise / concern    (rigid, unyielding)

8) (cute, attractive)    lovely / fine / very / pretty / ample    (moderately, quite)

9) (agreement, bond)    pledge / consume / decline / contract    (reduce, shrink)

10) (join, interact)    engage / launch / assault / covenant    (promise to marry)

# Connections 3

Difficulty Level: Medium
(Suggested completion time: 8 minutes)

Select the word from the group of words in the middle of the page, that has a similar meaning to the words listed in each of the brackets on the right and left sides.

1)  (enjoy, like)        fancy / vibe / relish / revel / salt / pepper        (sauce, condiment)

2)  (stain, blemish)        scar / image / spot / mark / brand        (impression, symbol)

3)  (solid, rigid)        hard / serious / dense / firm / thick        (tough, difficult)

4)  (lecture, sermon)        discourse / address / domicile / dwelling        (location, place)

5)  (ban, prohibit)        refuse / obstruct / clog / stake / bar        (rod, pole)

6)  (dance, reception)        promenade / balloon / ball / disco        (sphere, orb)

7)  (crypt, tomb)        dig / dour / grave / pit / vault / staid        (serious, grim)

8)  (replica, copy)        facsimile / imitation / model / atypical        (ideal, exemplary)

9)  (feature, characteristic)        facet / quirk / attribute / apply        (credit, associate with)

10)  (reduction, decrease)        rebate / discount / reject / minimize        (ignore, disregard)

# Connections 4

Difficulty Level: Medium
(Suggested completion time: 8 minutes)

Select the word from the group of words in the middle of the page, that has a similar meaning to the words listed in each of the brackets on the right and left sides.

1) (see, discover)          target / spot / observe / symbol          (mark, stain)

2) (lead, govern)          administration / key / rule / code          (regulation, law)

3) (present, donation)          offer / flair / gift / talent / charity          (ability, skill)

4) (chunk, slab)          piece / choke / block / jam / plug          (obstruct / barricade)

5) (leave, separate)          part / wedge / scrap / share / lump          (slice, portion)

6) (cliff, ridge)          slope / peak / hoax / bluff / sham          (deception, fake)

7) (pillar, post)          support / vertical / column / parade          (procession, convoy)

8) (passage, waterway)          radio / channel / vehicle / canal          (way of communicating)

9) (area of land)          profession / garden / pitch / field / degree          (area of interest)

10) (instructor, trainer)          guru / coach / car / tutor / cab          (carriage, wagon)

# Odd One Out 1

Difficulty Level: Easy
(Suggested completion time: 8 minutes)

Select the word form each group below that does not have the same general meaning, theme, classification or otherwise belong with the others.

Example:　　　green　　　blue　　　purple　　　teal　　　(lobster)

1)　oven　　kiln　　football　　furnace　　fire　　stove

2)　ferret　　elephant　　frog　　rock　　mouse　　butterfly

3)　read　　book　　newspaper　　magazine　　article　　comic

4)　uncomplicated　　simple　　complex　　easy　　straightforward

5)　enjoyable　　entertaining　　agreeable　　amusing　　disturbing

6)　tennis　　racquetball　　swimming　　rugby　　badminton

7)　helicopter　　jet　　plane　　spear　　spacecraft

8)　thin　　slender　　narrow　　skinny　　slim　　broad

9)　brother　　sister　　friend　　mother　　uncle　　cousin

10)　biscuit　　bread　　cake　　tart　　apple　　muffin

# Odd One Out 2

Difficulty Level: Easy/Medium
(Suggested completion time: 10 minutes)

Select the word form each group below that does not have the same general meaning, theme, classification or otherwise belong with the others.

1) gargantuan    towering    massive    colossal    minuscule

2) tangerine    pineapple    zucchini    raspberry    apple    pear

3) alien    outsider    foreign    stranger    native    visitor

4) jacket    vest    waistcoat    scarf    hoodie    T-shirt

5) crucial    vital    pivotal    impractical    integral

6) lamp    torch    shadow    spotlight    beam    lantern

7) finger    digit    number    hand    palm    thumb

8) surgery    syringe    drip    trickery    nurse    paramedic

9) ancient    old    prehistoric    contemporary    primitive

10) maths    chemistry    biology    physics    history

11) coin    button    ring    computer    tyre    ball

12) profound    funny    comical    amusing    humorous

# Odd One Out 3

Difficulty Level: Medium

(Suggested completion time: 10 minutes)

Select the word form each group below that does not have the same general meaning, theme, classification or otherwise belong with the others.

1) mystery    riddle    selection    enigma    question    uncertainty

2) lorry    bicycle    motorcycle    moped    bus    ambulance

3) catastrophe    disaster    fiasco    debacle    fortunate

4) litre    centimetre    tank    mile    gallon    stone    inch

5) head    chief    chair    table    president    ruler    captain

6) odour    smell    fragrance    cheese    whiff    aroma

7) cup    beaker    canteen    compass    chalice    vase

8) clear    transparent    obvious    ambiguous    open

9) rapid    swift    fast    glacial    prompt    speedy

10) corduroy    denim    satin    linen    leather    parka    silk

11) bungalow    cottage    mansion    palace    kiosk    igloo

12) twins    couple    pare    double    duet    pair

# Odd One Out 4

Difficulty Level: Medium

(Suggested completion time: 15 minutes)

Select the word form each group below that does not have the same general meaning, theme, classification or otherwise belong with the others.

1) cranium     nose     temple     abdomen     ear     jawbone

2) weak     feeble     anemic     potent     decrepit     infirm

3) radiant     bland     glistening     vivid     burnished     incandescent

4) perturbed     furious     baffled     indignant     incensed     livid

5) chisel     hammer     anvil     pliers     antenna     plane

6) elaborate     elegant     ornate     unsophisticated     sumptuous

7) square     rectangle     triangle     cube     polygon

8) scared     frightened     mesmerised     petrified     alarmed

9) lament     grieve     mourn     wail     savour     weep     agonise

10) flat     even     level     horizontal     lopsided     flush

11) leaf     petal     pencil     blade     stem     needle

12) emit     camouflage     disguise     mask     cover     conceal

# Odd One Out 5

Difficulty Level: Hard
(Suggested completion time: 10 minutes)

Select the word form each group below that does not have the same general meaning, theme, classification or otherwise belong with the others.

1)  conflict      battle      struggle      reconciliation      clash      row

2)  intellect      oblivion      acumen      savviness      comprehension

3)  resonate      boom      echo      blare      clang      toil      creak

4)  hairdresser      tailor      barrister      patron      reporter      banker

5)  journal      dictionary      exercise book      diary      workbook

6)  candlestick      matches      cardboard      mothball      tablespoon

7)  temperamental      fickle      unstable      enduring      volatile

8)  mandarin      nectarine      apricot      peach      plum

9)  wander      roam      ramble      stall      meander      drift

10)  repel      capitulate      thwart      repulse      foil      frustrate      resist

11)  gap      separation      difference      breach      union      split

12)  able      belt      deal      fair      give      heat      pure

# JUST FOR FUN

## Word Scramble

Find the answer to each of questions by looking at the picture clue and filling in the missing letters. Then answer the last question by using all the letters in the <u>boxes</u> only.

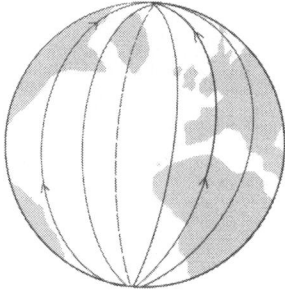

**1 inch = 1 mile (1 : 25,000)**

L ☐ N ☐ I T U D ☐

S C ☐ __ E

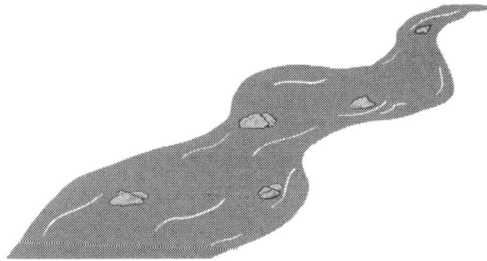

☐ I V E __

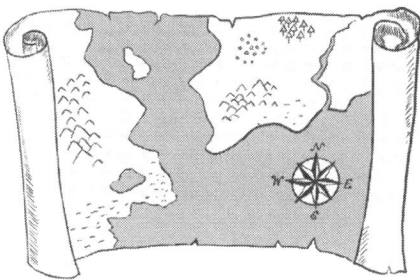

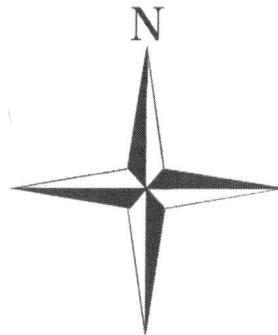

__ A ☐

N __ R __ ☐

What is the main theme of these words?

| | | | G | | | | Y |
|---|---|---|---|---|---|---|---|

65

# JUST FOR FUN
## Rebus Puzzles

A rebus is a clever combination of pictures, letters, numbers or words, that makes up an idea or saying – usually in a humorous way. Although they are not seen generally in exams, they are useful in helping you think more about visual clues and using logic to solve them. But more importantly, they can be quite fun!

Example:

SECRET
SECRET SECRET
SECRET SECRET SECRET

Answer: Top Secret

Example:

META    META

META    META

Answer: Metaphor (meta four times)

1)  TIME          abdefghijklmnopqrstuvwxyz

2)  B
    O W

3)  NOON good          4)  m11y l i1f1e

5)  lannnnguage          6)  CHAWHORWHOGE

7)  **arrest**
    *your*

8)  C
    C C C
    C C C C
    C CC C C
    C **ING** C

9)  R A D A N C I N G I N

10)
         10
    10  10  10
        2    10   10
              10
    10   10   10
          10     10
         10

11) *tougetch*

12) me     ...some1

13) Mary
+ Mary
_____

14) 

*Eleven Plus Vocabulary:*

15) b**9**     (hint: not harmful)

16) (12 − 2) a      (hint: persistence)

17) X       (hint: expensive)

18)       (hint: contradiction)

19)       (hint: vigorous)

20) $N$      (hint: encourage)

21) **a**   (hint: there's plenty)

*A bit of a laugh:*

22) T

23)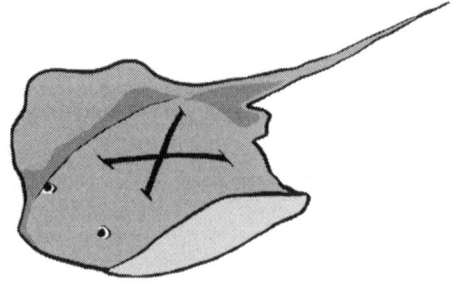

24) i **Aughhhh!**

25)

26)  Cluck Cluck *Honk! Honk!* Quack!

27)
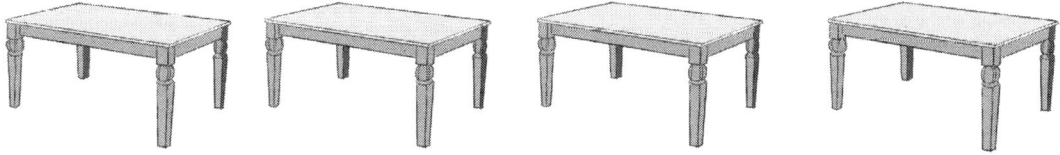

28)

29)

30)

31)

32)

# Complete the Word 1
Difficulty Level: Easy
(Suggested completion time: 5 minutes)

In these exercises, pick the 3-letter word from the choices given, that can be combined together with the underlined letters to form the right word to complete the sentence. The word may be inserted before, after, or in between the letters.

*Example: (Answer – **winter**)*

In the <u>TER</u> we like to go snowboarding and skiing in the mountains.

**SUN** **(WIN)** **SUM** **FOR** **OUT**

1) Laura's new <u>GFISH</u> has very large eyes.

**POP** **NAY** **OFT** **OLD** **PAD**

2) I can't <u>BEVE</u> that another year has gone by so quickly..

**LOT** **LIE** **RAN** **BIT** **FOR**

3) <u>DESE</u> losing her map, Evelyn was able to make it home safely.

**PIT** **PAW** **POT** **FOR** **SUN**

4) Darcy's cat caused trouble when she <u>FOLED</u> her to school.

**FAD** **FOR** **OIL** **LOW** **AND**

5) The <u>STERS</u> on Devan's house were painted blue.

**HAT** **HUT** **FIN** **DOG** **BIN**

6) Maria's brother is going to <u>AP</u> to university next year.

**TIN** **LOW** **LAP** **LIP** **PLY**

7) Gran likes to keep the sweets hidden in the <u>BOARD</u>.

**HAM** **EGG** **CUP** **OFF** **PAW**

8) Mum told me to not to let such <u>MI</u> problems bother me so much.

**LOT** **EAR** **MAN** **RUG** **NOR**

9) Uncle Ian will only buy high-quality <u>DEN</u> furniture.

**TAT** **SEA** **TIN** **WOO** **OLD**

10) Dad still has a <u>SUBSCTION</u> to the newspaper and reads it every evening.

**RAP** **RIP** **BUS** **RID** **TIN**

# Complete the Word 2

Difficulty Level: Medium
(Suggested completion time: 8 minutes)

In these exercises, pick the 3-letter word from the choices given, that can be combined together with the underlined letters to form the right word to complete the sentence.

1) Suddenly a flock of birds <u>EARED</u> in the sky.

**GIG      DIS      AYE      SUB      APP**

2) Mavis has started listening to <u>CASTS</u> in her spare time.

**POD      OUT      OLD      MID      FOR**

3) There is a <u>OUR</u> going around that a new headmaster is coming next month.

**TOO      VAL      RUM      DEV      MAD**

4) From the top of the tower, the people <u>BE</u> looked as small as ants.

**LIE      LOW      EYE      RAN      PAD**

5) There is fierce <u>COMITION</u> to make it into the Olympics.

**MOM      HAS      PIT      BIT      PET**

6) Giovanni plans to study maths and <u>CISTRY</u> for his A levels.

**HEM      MIN      CUT      TOT      HIM**

7) Isabella was surprised that she felt so comfortable in her new <u>SURROUNGS</u>.

**GIN      DOT      DIN      ABS      TOP**

8) Ben was <u>FAL</u> with his finances, so he had plenty of money to go on holiday.

**LOW      EAR      POP      RUG      BUG**

9) Scientists are looking for more <u>SUSTAILE</u> ways of producing energy.

**SUN      NAB      BUT      FOR      AND**

10) The Bayeux <u>TAPES</u> is a representation of the invasion of England in 1066.

**BET      TRY      DUO      BOT      FAD**

11) Florian has always wanted to see the great <u>PYRAS</u> of Egypt.

**MAD      TON      LOG      MID      POD**

12) The Industrial Revolution <u>CONTRIED</u> to a rise in population in the 1800s.

**CAN      BUT      LOW      OUT      BIT**

# Complete the Word 3

Difficulty Level: Medium/Hard
(Suggested completion time: 10 minutes)

In these exercises, pick the 3-letter word from the choices given, that can be combined with the underlined letters to form the right word to complete the sentence.

1) Petunias and lavender are two types of flowers that FLISH in the sunlight.

   **OWN**    **FIT**    **OWL**    **OUR**    **ONE**

2) The meeting was ADJNED until January 14.

   **ODD**    **ORE**    **ONE**    **OWN**    **OUR**

3) Stuart was AMUOUS about when he would be able to come to the party.

   **OUT**    **FIB**    **GYM**    **BIG**    **BUN**

4) Shawn tried to VINCE his friends that he was a distant relative to the King.

   **THY**    **CON**    **OFT**    **DAB**    **GEE**

5) The singer dressed in a FLAMANT style which was appreciated by his fans.

   **DUO**    **TOO**    **PHI**    **BOY**    **SLY**

6) Norma was EXASPEED at her little brother's non-stop moaning.

   **AWE**    **DIP**    **MAD**    **WRY**    **RAT**

7) Emily estimated a POTIAL earnings of 1000 pounds per week with her new store.

   **TIN**    **WHO**    **TEN**    **IMP**    **DEF**

8) We have been completely open and TSPARENT in our negotiations.

   **RAN**    **ARM**    **ION**    **TAT**    **YET**

9) With a little help from her friends, Ari MAND to get home safely.

   **VIE**    **AGE**    **ROW**    **BIN**    **LOT**

10) Hailey was surprised at how GESQUE some of the Halloween masks were.

   **ROT**    **REP**    **ROB**    **REM**    **ROE**

11) A weekend off APLED to Tina after two months of hard work.

   **GAP**    **POT**    **PRO**    **PEA**    **PIE**

12) The money was transported from the bank in an OURED vehicle.

   **WAX**    **ARM**    **AIM**    **TOM**    **RUM**

# Complete the Word 4

In these exercises, pick the 3-letter word from the choices given, that can be combined with the underlined letters to form the right word to complete the sentence.

1) Mr. Morris would not <u>COND</u> inappropriate behaviour in the classroom.

    **FAN**    **WIT**    **TON**    **DID**    **ONE**

2) Marco was <u>LORN</u> after his best friend moved to Australia.

    **COD**    **ADO**    **FOR**    **DIN**    **MAC**

3) Danielle glided through the obstacle course with great <u>ESSE</u>.

    **PEG**    **FIN**    **OLE**    **SOW**    **TOM**

4) The small town was heavily damaged by the <u>ING</u> storm.

    **CAR**    **TIP**    **TON**    **TAX**    **RAG**

5) The journey up the hill was long and <u>ARUS</u>.

    **DUO**    **VOW**    **TED**    **SUN**    **OPT**

6) The army achieved the <u>ELET</u> of surprise by arriving a day earlier than anticipated.

    **MAN**    **LAM**    **DYE**    **MEN**    **ALT**

7) Mel does not like <u>CDS</u>, so she avoids going into the city centre.

    **FOR**    **ARM**    **ROW**    **OFF**    **OUR**

8) We are going to <u>COME</u> in the netball tournament this weekend.

    **AWE**    **OUT**    **VET**    **PET**    **WEL**

9) It was Cedric's <u>AMION</u> to win the Nobel Prize before he turned forty.

    **AIM**    **HER**    **CON**    **BIS**    **BIT**

10) No one seemed to <u>NOT</u> the dolphins playing at sunset.

    **HIP**    **ACE**    **ICE**    **ANY**    **FOR**

11) Bill told us a funny <u>ANECE</u> about the time he got lost in the chocolate factory.

    **GEM**    **ORB**    **DOT**    **FUN**    **RIB**

12) Molly was <u>INNANT</u> when the teacher accused her of cheating on the test.

    **DAY**    **LIB**    **RED**    **SAG**    **DIG**

# Complete the Word 5

Difficulty Level: Hard
(Suggested completion time: 10 minutes)

In these exercises, pick the 4-letter word from the choices given, that can be combined with the underlined letters to form the right word to complete the sentence.

1) Nelson's IRRENT attitude landed him in trouble quite often.

   **RATE**   **TANK**   **KIND**   **EVER**   **TALL**

2) In the warm summer evening we enjoy a LEILY stroll by the river.

   **SURE**   **SEPT**   **EARN**   **AREA**   **ONTO**

3) Laura's mother is a PRONT psychiatrist who lectures at Cambridge.

   **USER**   **LINE**   **EDGE**   **TILL**   **MINE**

4) Wishing not to PRO the ordeal, he apologised and left immediately.

   **DATE**   **MEAN**   **SHUT**   **LONG**   **MISS**

5) We had to DE the tent from a swarm of angry hornets.

   **SIGN**   **FEAT**   **VOID**   **PART**   **FEND**

6) When it came to the washing up, Joe was extremely AETIC.

   **PATH**   **BANK**   **PILL**   **OVER**   **SEND**

7) The sloth is a SEARY creature that sleeps 15-20 hours a day.

   **ONTO**   **DIET**   **DENT**   **CROP**   **ARMY**

8) That odour in the cellar is NAUING.

   **YEAH**   **SOLE**   **SIGN**   **SEAL**   **SEAT**

9) The company EXED my contract for another year.

   **TOLD**   **TEND**   **TOOK**   **TEST**   **TERM**

10) Thom's BICKE ruined what had been otherwise a pleasant evening out.

   **SAKE**   **ROLL**   **RING**   **MOOD**   **PASS**

11) When he was ill, Hugo was COND to his bedroom.

   **FINE**   **FORM**   **DENY**   **HURT**   **FATE**

12) The mansion was the official RENCE of the ambassador.

   **CARE**   **AREA**   **PARK**   **SIDE**   **RING**

# JUST FOR PUN – PART II

I just wrote a ballad about tortillas, chicken and rice.

Wouldn't it be better as a rap?

---

What do you call a smelly gentleman who likes to tell puns?

A **pun-gent**!

---

What happened? You were really slow today. Way off your best.

I was so hungry during the race, so I just ate my watch.

Did you really eat a watch?

Yes, and it was very time-consuming.

What do you call an alligator in a vest?

- An investigator

§

How do you know when a clock is starving?

- It goes back four seconds

§

Which dinosaur was the most literate?

- The Thesaurus

You're the gratest

You're smug

# JUST FOR FUN
## Cloze Word Search

Find the words in the puzzle from the clues below. What is the common theme of all of the words?

1) A distinct smell        A ☐ O ☐ A

2) A loud collection of noises        ☐ A C O ☐ H O ☐ ☐

3) dark and dirty, cannot be seen through        M ☐ R K ☐

4) having a strong taste or smell        ☐ U N ☐ E N ☐

5) having a rough texture        C ☐ A ☐ S ☐

6) tangy, usually hot tasting        ☐ P I ☐ Y

7) feeling slightly wet        ☐ A ☐ P

8) describing intense or bright colours        V ☐ V ☐ D

| V | C | A | C | O | P | H | N | O | N | M | R | O |
|---|---|---|---|---|---|---|---|---|---|---|---|---|
| I | A | P | A | U | R | Y | E | Y | K | R | U | M |
| D | C | A | C | O | C | P | S | K | R | M | K | A |
| V | P | M | O | I | T | U | E | S | R | U | O | C |
| I | H | O | P | U | N | G | E | N | T | O | R | A |
| V | Y | S | H | S | G | Y | D | P | U | M | R | V |
| I | N | C | O | A | R | S | E | A | I | O | A | I |
| D | A | P | N | T | N | P | V | C | M | E | D | V |
| O | R | R | Y | S | E | N | Y | A | L | P | M | I |

Words can be found forwards, backwards, up, down, or diagonally

What do all of these words relate to?

Answer: **S** ☐ ☐ **S** ☐ **S**

76

# MISSING LETTER SENTENCES 1

Difficulty Level: Easy
(Suggested completion time: 8 minutes)

Fill in the missing letters to complete the sentence. Use the context of the sentence to help find the right word and spelling.

1. The teacher showed Harry's work as an **e**☐☐☐**ple** of great writing.

2. We ☐☐☐**ited** our uncle for lunch on Saturday.

3. The ruler **de**☐☐☐**ed** that the people should pay a tax.

4. **F**☐☐☐**us** actors are often recognised when they go out.

5. Healthy eating and **ex**☐☐☐**ise** will keep you fit.

6. The team are **trai**☐☐☐**g** for the competition.

7. Right is the **op**☐☐☐**ite** of left.

8. It is a ☐☐☐**me** that Robbie missed the concert.

9. My **fa**☐☐☐**rite** style of music is Hip Hop.

10. The children received **th**☐**i**☐ certificates.

11. I can't decide which to ☐☐☐**ose**.

12. The Scottish Highlands are an amazing ☐☐☐**ht**.

13. The **c**☐☐☐**ate** in a rainforest is hot and humid.

14. It is hard to **im**☐☐☐**ne** life without the internet these days.

15. Ari's new **c**☐☐☐**ra** has some smart features.

# MISSING LETTER SENTENCES 2

### Difficulty Level: Easy
### (Suggested completion time: 8 minutes)

Fill in the missing letters to complete the sentence. Use the context of the sentence to help find the right word and spelling.

1.  I **dre**[ ][ ][ ] of winning a million pounds last night.

2.  The salesman assured the customer that the **q**[ ][ ][ ]**ity** of the product was exceptional.

3.  Sam was happy to [ ][ ][ ]**ch** the end of the test.

4.  Liz hates the [ ][ ][ ]**te** of avocadoes!

5.  We should plan to go to **the**[ ][ ]**re** today.

6.  Lottie received a **p**[ ][ ][ ]**e** for the story she entered in the competition.

7.  The **bro**[ ][ ][ ] chair could not be restored.

8.  At the seaside, Mum ate the 'C[ ][ ][ ]**h** of the Day'.

9.  'W[ ][ ][ ]**h** do you prefer?'

10. Nicky had fun at the **a**[ ][ ][ ]**ement** arcade.

11. 'Give me a **m**[ ][ ][ ]**nt**. I'm not ready yet.'

12. N[ ][ ][ ]**dy** was out because of the bad weather.

13. The **pi**[ ][ ][ ]**re** was hung carefully on the wall.

14. The captain **li**[ ][ ][ ]**d** the trophy with glee.

15. The poor man had to chase his playful dog [ ][ ][ ]**und** the block twice.

# MISSING LETTER SENTENCES 3

Difficulty Level: Easy
(Suggested completion time: 8 minutes)

Fill in the missing letters to complete the sentence. Use the context of the sentence to help find the right word and spelling.

1.   You should make your bed ☐☐☐**ry** day.

2.   The sign ☐☐☐**nted** to the left.

3.   Marigolds are a **t**☐☐☐ of flower.

4.   Are you **s**☐☐☐ that is right?

5.   The scene before them was **b**☐☐☐**tiful**.

6.   **S**☐**ar**☐ knives are very dangerous.

7.   This climb is particularly ☐☐☐**ep**.

8.   Young Kim was very **p**☐**ou**☐ when he learnt to tie his shoelaces.

9.   The class spent days preparing for the **s**☐**e**☐**ia**☐ event.

10.  The ☐☐**rg**☐ suitcase was difficult to carry.

11.  The **sp**☐**c**☐**cra**☐**t** would land soon.

12.  The **j**☐☐**r**☐**ey** was long and tiring.

13.  I would like to be an ☐**ut**☐☐**r** and write many books.

14.  Rish likes to be outside and spends many hours **ga**☐**d**☐**nin**☐.

15.  Maisy **s**☐**r**☐**a**☐ the blanket out on the grass for the picnic.

# MISSING LETTER SENTENCES 4

Difficulty Level: Medium
(Suggested completion time: 10 minutes)

Fill in the missing letters to complete the sentence. Use the context of the sentence to help find the right word and spelling.

1.  The expert tried to ☐☐☐ **tore** the ancient monument to its former glory.

2.  Charles Dickens wrote the **n**☐☐☐**l** 'Oliver Twist'.

3.  The **b**☐☐☐**e** made its way along the canal.

4.  It is difficult to play on a very wet football ☐☐☐**ch**.

5.  There was a **def**☐☐**t** with the machinery, so it did not work.

6.  If you want to know the wind direction, check a weather **v**☐☐**e**.

7.  Moss had a **ph**☐☐☐**a** about snakes but loved lizards.

8.  It is difficult to see in the ☐☐☐**ky** water.

9.  You should ☐☐☐**l** '999' in an emergency.

10. A tornado can cause **se**☐☐☐**e** damage to trees and homes.

11. Ruby had a **stom**☐☐☐ ache on Saturday.

12. The **n**☐☐☐ lights shone brightly at night in the big city.

13. The gymnast was extremely **n**☐☐☐**le**.

14. The architect decided to **al**☐☐☐ the plans.

15. The hikers used a **comp**☐☐☐ to work out the correct direction.

# MISSING LETTER SENTENCES 5

Difficulty Level: Medium
(Suggested completion time: 10 minutes)

Fill in the missing letters to complete the sentence. Use the context of the sentence to help find the right word and spelling.

1. To find the area of a rectangle, multiply the height by the **wi**▢▢▢ .

2. The suspect had some **distin**▢▢▢**shing** features.

3. Keep away from a **s**▢▢▢**m** of wasps.

4. Coal mining was an important **i**▢▢▢**stry** in the 19th century and is still used today.

5. **Jew**▢▢▢**ery** such as earrings and necklaces are often beautifully made.

6. The **cel**▢▢▢ was cold and damp.

7. The writing on the old manuscript was very **f**▢▢▢**t**.

8. Henry VIII had many **ban**▢▢▢**ts** at Hampton Court.

9. The **tem**▢▢▢**ature** was very mild for January.

10. Frogs and toads are **amp**▢▢▢**ians**.

11. The **b**▢▢▢**ing** was hung for the jubilee celebration.

12. If something is beyond monetary value, we say it is **p**▢▢▢**eless**.

13. **Cons**▢▢▢ a doctor if you are very unwell.

14. **S**▢▢▢**t** is mixture of rain with snow.

15. The **f**▢▢▢**t** of ships reached the harbour.

# MISSING LETTER SENTENCES 6

### Difficulty Level: Medium
### (Suggested completion time: 10 minutes)

Fill in the missing letters to complete the sentence. Use the context of the sentence to help find the right word and spelling.

1. **F**☐☐☐ your clothes before putting them in a drawer.

2. The king **re**☐☐☐**ed** for 20 years.

3. The countryside is often called **ru**☐☐☐.

4. At ☐☐☐**k** the sun set.

5. The drummer played with excellent **rhy**☐☐☐.

6. Cassie was **extr**☐☐☐**ly** excited about the party.

7. The gardener grew **tom**☐☐☐**es** in her greenhouse.

8. It is **ne**☐☐☐**sary** to follow the rules at the swimming pool.

9. **Pop**☐☐☐**r** fashions come and go.

10. The ☐☐☐**ience** clapped loudly.

11. Tara had ☐☐☐**ugh** money for some stationery.

12. It is ☐☐☐**sual** to have snow in May, but it's not impossible.

13. A **leo**☐☐☐**d** is a member of the cat family.

14. It is good to train before climbing a **mount**☐☐☐.

15. A **t**☐☐☐**inal** is used for flight and bus departures.

# MISSING LETTER SENTENCES 7

## Difficulty Level: Hard
### (Suggested completion time: 10 minutes)

Fill in the missing letters to complete the sentence. Use the context of the sentence to help find the right word and spelling.

1. There was an **a**☐☐**nd**☐**nc**☐ of gifts for the new baby.

2. Maggie was **ap**☐**rehen**☐☐**ve** about the test.

3. The team felt ☐☐☐**mal** after the loss.

4. The man had been a **dire**☐☐☐**r** at the old factory for a long time.

5. A shape such as a spiral is a **h**☐**l**☐**x**.

6. Wealthy people sometimes live a **l**☐**vi**☐**h** lifestyle.

7. Micky had his teeth straightened by the ☐☐☐**hodontist**.

8. The question **per**☐**le**☐☐**d** Harvey.

9. The holiday ☐☐**s**☐**rt** was over-crowed on the very hot day.

10. Morgan enjoyed wearing a **u**☐☐☐**orm** to work.

11. Mia ☐**o**☐☐**d** the bandage around his arm.

12. The villagers lived in small **dw**☐☐☐**ings** beside the river.

13. Stay **a**☐☐☐**t** when crossing the road.

14. We **be**☐☐☐**it** when we learn from our mistakes.

15. The logs were **c**☐**a**☐☐**ed** by the fire.

# MISSING LETTER SENTENCES 8

Difficulty Level: Hard
(Suggested completion time: 10 minutes)

Fill in the missing letters to complete the sentence. Use the context of the sentence to help find the right word and spelling.

1.  The children were surprised by the **del**☐☐**er**☐☐**e** mistake.

2.  The building must be ☐**emo**☐**i**☐**hed** because it is dangerous.

3.  A beautiful butterfly ☐**me**☐☐**ed** from the cocoon.

4.  The artist was very ☐☐☐**ble** about her abilities.

5.  ☐☐☐**via** is not important, but sometimes fun to know.

6.  Rory found the steep ☐☐☐**pe** particularly treacherous when skiing.

7.  The answer was quite **ob**☐☐☐**re** and difficult to find.

8.  The opposite of expand is **co**☐☐**ra**☐**t.**

9.  The suspect tried to ☐☐☐**e** the scene of the crime.

10. There is a water shortage, and the town is suffering from a **dr**☐☐☐**ht.**

11. We must care for the **h**☐☐**ita**☐**s** of endangered species.

12. The **anti**☐☐☐**s** were very old and expensive.

13. The peak of a mountain is the ☐☐☐**mit.**

14. **S**☐☐☐**dy** boots help when climbing.

15. The dinosaurs faced ☐**x**☐**in**☐**tion** thousands of years ago.

# MISSING LETTER SENTENCES 9

Fill in the missing letters to complete the sentence. Use the context of the sentence to help find the right word and spelling.

1.  The **tra**☐☐**ui**☐ beach was a lovely place to rest.

2.  Harry complained that his big sister **to**☐☐**en**☐**ed** him.

3.  The horse **pul**☐☐☐ the cart down the road.

4.  Do not stand too close to the ☐☐**r**☐ when you intend to cross the road.

5.  We were **ta**☐☐☐**t** our times tables at school.

6.  The thief got away with the **l**☐☐☐!

7.  Pigs often feed from a **t**☐☐**u**☐**h**.

8.  Remi decided to **re**☐☐☐**re** the old furniture.

9.  Flo read an interesting magazine ☐☐☐**icle**.

10. A **pl**☐☐☐**er** fixed the pipes.

11. The suspect had an ☐☐☐**bi**, so it wasn't him.

12. The entire **c**☐☐☐ performed wonderfully in the play.

13. The teacher was **f**☐☐☐ but fair.

14. Suzie wore her hair in a **pl**☐☐☐.

15. Cats are described as **fe**☐☐☐**e**.

# JUST FOR FUN
## Cloze Word Search

Find the words in the puzzle from the clues below. What is the common theme of all of the words?

1) The force that keeps us on earth ☐ R ☐ V ☐ T ☐

2) A point of light in the night sky ☐ ☐ ☐ R

3) A group of stars ☐ O ☐ S ☐ E L ☐ ☐ T ☐ ☐ N

4) It makes distant things appear closer ☐ ☐ L ☐ S ☐ O ☐ E

5) This orbits the Earth ☐ O ☐ N

6) The biggest planet in our galaxy ☐ ☐ P ☐ ☐ E ☐

7) It's really everything there is ☐ N ☐ V ☐ R ☐ ☐

8) The last planet discovered*; Mickey Mouse's dog ☐ L ☐ ☐ O
   * later classified as a 'dwarf planet'

```
B G M R E T I P U J G E W
E R U Y U S A T T U L P A
C O N S T E L L A T I O N
P J I M A I R O Y R G C P
L U V O M D V E R A T S L
A P E D O W L A N F E E U
N L R Y O S I M R S O L T
D A S O N G V Q I G H E O
C R E I O R E T S A C T Q
```

Words can be found forwards, backwards, up, down, or diagonally

What is the common theme of all the clues?

Answer: ☐ S ☐ O ☐ ☐ M ☐

86

# JUST FOR FUN
## Word Themes

Match the words on the left to the categories on the right where they fit best. Some words may fit in more than one, but there should be at least **four** words per category.

lecture

apparel

entrée

whiteboard

savoury

tools

curriculum

cuisine

stethoscope

hardware

antiseptic

escalator

blazer

literacy

gauze

appetiser

textiles

utensils

rubber        diagnosis

hinges

jewellery

**Department Store**

**Doctor's Surgery**

**Education/ Classroom**

**Restaurant**

**Ironmonger**

# MISSING WORDS 1

Difficulty Level: Easy
(Suggested completion time: 10 minutes)

Use the word bank to complete the sentences. Words can only be used once.

| | | | | |
|---|---|---|---|---|
| volatile | sombre | sauntered | prosperous | forecast |
| sabre | composer | lethargic | obscured | thaw |
| distress | violet | drab | draft | jovial |
| chords | terminal | swell | | |

1. There was a long queue at the airport _____.

2. The _____ was elated with his new musical score.

3. Conversations were very _____ at the funeral.

4. The glare of another car's headlights _____ the driver's view of the road.

5. Tami's finger began to _____ and the bruising turned a shade of _____ .

6. George strummed some _____ on his guitar.

7. The situation was _____ as the soldiers held their positions in the desert.

8. The young lad _____ down the street, as if he had no cares in the world.

9. Rich was in a _____ mood because his business was very _____ .

10. The editor looked at the _____ and decided there were too many words.

11. Viv was feeling too _____ to whisk the ingredients adequately.

12. Mel was in _____ because she forgot to buy her sister a present.

13. The _____ called for moderate temperatures throughout the day.

14. Mum put the frozen chicken in the microwave to _____.

15. Gabriel changed his _____ bedroom into a bright and cheerful space.

16. In the museum was saw an old _____ that belonged to Wellington.

# MISSING WORDS 2
## Difficulty Level: Medium
### (Suggested completion time: 12 minutes)

Use the word bank to complete the sentences. Words can only be used once.

| | | | | |
|---|---|---|---|---|
| elapsed | alibi | globe | source | dense |
| orchard | reservoir | generation | coax | artifacts |
| cargo | support | barge | friar | chevron |
| strewn | forgo | embarked | decorating | |
| released | bare | nervous | clothing | |

1. The _____ carried the _____ along the canal to the port.

2. The explorer discovered many _____ as she travelled the across the _____.

3. The chair of the committee was non-committal when asked if he would _____ the proposal.

4. Many people like _____ patterns and use them for _____ .

5. _____ was _____ about the bedroom by the untidy child.

6. The field was previously a fruitful _____ but was laid _____ since the drought.

7. The suspect had an _____ for the crime and was _____ .

8. The _____ lived in an abbey hidden by a _____ forest.

9. Our community uses the clean water _____ of the _____ .

10. A long time has _____ since the older _____ fought in the war.

11. We tried to _____ the rabbit out of his burrow, but he was too _____.

12. Harry decided to _____ most chocolate, as he _____ on a plan of a healthy diet.

# MISSING WORDS 3

Difficulty Level: Medium
(Suggested completion time: 12 minutes)

Use the word bank to complete the sentences. Words can only be used once.

| | | | | |
|---|---|---|---|---|
| generous | aimlessly | meagre | reverse | sponsored |
| adjust | dainty | yearned | extracted | current |
| pondered | chilly | solution | opposite | courteous |
| obedient | errors | cultures | biased | faint |
| fragile | gloomy | distracted | reliant | |

1. Many friends and family were _____ when Clark embarked upon a _____ walk.

2. As the river _____ was very fast, the rowers were _____ upon each other to reach safety.

3. Molly enjoyed creating _____ doodles when she was _____ in class.

4. The morning was _____ yet sunny.  Unfortunately, the forecast for the afternoon was _____.

5. Tom carefully _____ the instrument from the box as it was _____ .

6. Sally's savings were _____, and she _____ upon just how she could  improve them.

7. The judges felt the decision was _____ and decided to _____ it.

8. The _____ to the problem was the _____ of what Ollie expected.

9. Servants in Victorian Britain were expected to be _____ and _____ in wealthy households, even if they were treated poorly.

10. Charlie wandered _____ as he _____ for some excitement.

11. When people from different _____ meet for the first time, there are sometimes _____ in communication.

12. Patti drew her design with _____ lines, in case she needed to _____ it.

# MISSING WORDS 4

Difficulty Level: Hard
(Suggested completion time: 15 minutes)

Use the word bank to complete the sentences. Words can only be used once.

| | | | | |
|---|---|---|---|---|
| engaged | strength | desirable | mesmerising | capital |
| thrifty | delicate | callous | descent | witty |
| hamper | rigid | boisterous | ancient | perplexing |
| exotic | humid | occupation | revealed | diluted |
| hostile | aloof | innocent | mend | |

1. The _____ lady chose to _____ her shoes in order to avoid needing new ones.

2. The _____ of Italy, Rome, is an _____ city.

3. The infants were _____ as they _____ in the playground  activities.

4. The morning haze _____ the _____ of the sun as Taylor drove through the countryside.

5. The _____ _____ crowd were angered by the _____ rules.

6. The mountaineer didn't let fear _____ his _____ .

7. Singapore is very _____ throughout the day, and the gardens are bursting with many _____ flowers.

8. The _____ of a comedian requires them to be extremely _____ .

9. The evidence _____ that the suspect was _____ .

10. This exquisite necklace is _____ and highly _____ .

11. The children found the magician _____ as they could not work out the _____ tricks.

12. The wealthy old lady sometimes appeared _____, but she was never _____ and was kind at heart.

# MISSING WORDS 5

Difficulty Level: Hard
(Suggested completion time: 15 minutes)

Use the word bank to complete the sentences. Words can only be used once.

| | | | | |
|---|---|---|---|---|
| collision | prohibited | enclosures | crumble | vapour |
| prominent | illusions | congestion | nourishment | investigate |
| debris | complimented | dwelling | complemented | apprentice |
| remorse | forthcoming | quaint | hapless | lenient |
| assortment | portrait | disastrous | entertained | |

1. The _____ waiter dropped the plate with _____ consequences.

2. After the factory exploded, _____ lay everywhere and a toxic _____ hung in the air.

3. The rescue workers provided an _____ of supplies and foods which offered _____ after the floods.

4. The police decided to _____ the incident, in which a _____ figure had been kidnapped.

5. The critic _____ the artist on his intricate _____ of the old lady.

6. Jess felt that the cold ice cream _____ the warm apple _____ very well.

7. The magician _____ his audience with clever _____.

8. The judge was more _____ when the defendant showed _____.

9. The Morris family enjoyed _____ in the _____ cottage during the summer.

10. The _____ was not _____ about his mistake which annoyed his employer greatly.

11. The _____ caused serious _____ on the motorway.

12. It is _____ to enter _____ at the zoo.

92

# JUST FOR FUN
## Word Scramble

Find the answer to each of questions by looking at the picture clue and filling in the missing letters. Then answer the last question by using all the letters in the boxes.

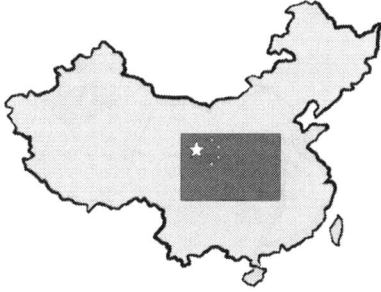

C ☐ ☐ N A

_ U ☐ L _ R Y

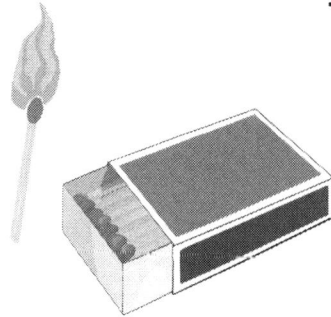

M _ T _ H ☐ S

C O L A ☐ D E _

☐ L _ C ☐

Where might you find all of these words?

☐ ☐ ☐ ☐ ☐ ☐ ☐

# Cloze Passages
Difficulty Level: Medium to Hard
(Suggested completion time: 15 minutes each)

In the following section you will be given several different passages. In each there will be missing words. Some will have a word bank, others will have options for each blank, where you must choose the right word. In two of the passages, you will have to provide the antonym of the word given.

These types of exercises test not only vocabulary and spelling, but require students to analyse and understand the text. We have provided a variety of text types in this section.

These exercises should help improve your ability to select the correct word in the right context. Each passage should take no more than <u>ten</u> <u>minutes</u> to complete.

## Heathrow Airport

London has six airports serving the greater metropolitan area. Heathrow Airport, located twenty-three _____**1**_____ west of central London, is not only the largest of these airports, but the biggest in the country and one of the largest in _____**2**_____.

Although it began as a small _____**3**_____ airport, Heathrow grew quickly after the end of the Second World War. Opening in 1946 simply as London Airport, in 1966 it was _____**4**_____ Heathrow Airport, after the _____**5**_____ on which it was built.

In the first year of _____**6**_____, Heathrow had approximately 63,000 passengers. As airline travel became more _____**7**_____, flights increased dramatically. In 2018, it was _____**8**_____ around 80 million passengers a year – more than the population of the United Kingdom.

Flights from Heathrow Airport _____**9**_____ travel to 203 cities in 84 countries all over the world. The most popular destinations are New York, Dubai, Dublin, Amsterdam, and Hong Kong. The _____**10**_____ flight at present from the airport is to Darwin, Australia, a total of 13,873 kilometres – lasting over sixteen hours!

Currently there are four _____**11**_____ in operation at Heathrow. Terminal 2, also known as 'The Queen's Terminal' was reopened in 2014. Terminal 5 is the busiest at Heathrow. Opened in 2008, it is _____**12**_____ mostly to British Airways flights.

In the 1950s, Heathrow operated six _____**13**_____. Today, only two are in operation – one for flights landing, one for flights departing. A third runway was approved after much _____**14**_____ and legal opposition, but as of 2022 had not been completed.

London's other major airports include London City, Stansted, _____**15**_____, Luton, and Southend.

Fill in the missing words in the passage below.

**Word Bank:** originated, association, tapestries, mythical, healing, spiralling, refer, representative, symbol, portrayed, ancient, reputation, purity, depicted, accessible

## Unicorns

The unicorn – the \_\_\_\_**1**\_\_\_\_ horse-like creature with a single, \_\_\_\_**2**\_\_\_\_ horn – is more popular today than perhaps it ever was. Although its \_\_\_\_**3**\_\_\_\_ is one of great rarity, it can be found virtually everywhere today on t-shirts, posters, television, literature, cartoons, foods, drinks, as well as toys.

The unicorn concept \_\_\_\_**4**\_\_\_\_ from the Bronze Age (3300 – 1200 B.C.) and looked more like a cow with a single horn. Indeed, the \_\_\_\_**5**\_\_\_\_ Greeks believed that the unicorn was not a myth, but an actual type of animal that lived in Asia.

In medieval times, the legend of the unicorn was captured in various \_\_\_\_**6**\_\_\_\_ and paintings, \_\_\_\_**7**\_\_\_\_ more as a combination of a goat and horse, white in colour with a single horn. The unicorn itself became a sign of \_\_\_\_**8**\_\_\_\_ and strength. Its singular horn was believed to have magical powers of \_\_\_\_**9**\_\_\_\_, so it was hunted for this trophy – as the legend grew. The tusk of the narwhal, an arctic whale, was sometimes passed off as being a real unicorn horn during this time.

The power and myth of the unicorn was so strong, that it even became a national \_\_\_\_**10**\_\_\_\_ of Scotland, being adopted by the King from around the 12th Century. The unicorn appeared on coins, statues, and other carvings. In the 1707 union of England and Scotland, the royal coat of arms \_\_\_\_**11**\_\_\_\_ the Unicorn as \_\_\_\_**12**\_\_\_\_ of Scotland. The unicorn remains today on the royal coat of arms of King Charles III.

In popular culture, the unicorn has appeared in books by C.S. Lewis and J. K. Rowling, as well as television programmes and movies. The \_\_\_\_**13**\_\_\_\_ of rainbows and unicorns is a more recent development in the unicorn legend. Perhaps to make unicorns more \_\_\_\_**14**\_\_\_\_ to children, the colours of the rainbow give a friendlier, and more fun and playful look to the unicorn. However, rainbows, like the unicorn, are also connected with magic. The term 'unicorn' is also used today to \_\_\_\_**15**\_\_\_\_ to something very rare.

Fill in the missing words in the passage below.

**Word Bank:** events, beacon, inhabited, graduates, united, spacious, industries, residence, seat, cultural, focal, insurance, destination, series, nicknamed

# Edinburgh

Situated in south-eastern Scotland on the Firth of Forth, Edinburgh is the capital and second-largest city in Scotland. Its rich history and importance as a ___**1**___ centre have made it a popular ___**2**___ for tourists from all over the world.

Edinburgh has been ___**3**___ for thousands of years, but gradually emerged as an important city as Scotland became an independent kingdom in the 1400s. Its population grew and it was a central part of historical ___**4**___ in Scotland until the Treaty of Union in 1706, which ___**5**___ Scotland and England into Great Britain. Today, it is the ___**6**___ of the Scottish Parliament and the high courts of Scotland.

The centre of the city is divided between and Old and New Town. Edinburgh Castle, rising high above the city on Castle Rock, is a dominant ___**7**___ point of the Old Town. A ___**8**___ of streets called The Royal Mile lead from the castle to Holyrood Palace, the official ___**9**___ of the British monarch in Scotland. New Town, which was built between the late 1700s and mid-1800s, was designed in the Georgian style, with wide streets and large, ___**10**___ houses.

Banking and ___**11**___ have been major ___**12**___ in Edinburgh since the 1800s. Research, education and tourism are also important – after London, Edinburgh is the most visited city in the United Kingdom.

Edinburgh has been ___**13**___ the 'Athens of the North' for its physical and similarities to the ancient Greek city. As a ___**14**___ of arts and culture, Edinburgh is host to the Scottish National Gallery, the Edinburgh International Festival, and the Fringe – widely recognised as the world's largest arts festival. The University of Edinburgh, established in 1582, is considered one of the finest universities in the world, with distinguished ___**15**___ such as Charles Darwin and Alexander Graham Bell.

# Cheltenham Literature Festival

What do Benedict Cumberbatch, Joe Wicks, Toni Morrison, Michael Palin, Salman Rushdie, Patrick Stewart, Andrew Lloyd Webber, David Cameron and Tom Daley have in common? They have all been special **(guests / events)** at the Times and Sunday Times Cheltenham Literature Festival!

For ten days in October, the Regency town of Cheltenham is host to the **(oldest / newest)** literature festival in the world. Founded in 1949, it has grown to become an internationally **(hosted / recognised)** event. It regularly **(refines / attracts / detracts)** new and best-selling authors, poets, and other celebrities.

Although the focus is literature, celebrating the written and **(spoken / digital)** word, there are plenty of discussions and **(debates / arguments)** on a variety of topics, and something for everyone to enjoy. In 2021, a three-year festival theme was introduced, called 'Read the World,' to encourage a wider **(range / mean)** of international authors and issues.

The festival is **(only / primarily)** based in Montpellier Gardens, which lies very close to the town centre. Some of the larger events are held in other **(venues / festivals)**, for example the Town Hall or at Cheltenham Racecourse. The main **(idea / location)** offers plenty of choices for food and drink, and with so many events to choose from, the festival **(affords / dispatches)** a perfect day out for everyone.

Although some of the events require tickets, **(their / there / they're)** are numerous free presentations and **(workshops / laboratories)**, particularly for families with children. The 2021 Festival featured two hundred free events and activities. During the **(pandemic / continuum)** in 2020, the festival received **(blame / acclaim)** for its combination of in-person and online events.

The Literature Festival is part of Cheltenham Festivals, which includes a Jazz, Science and Music Festival, as well as a charity that provides educational and talent development programmes.

## The Praying Mantis

Named for the way they hold their **(front / hind)** legs – bent forward as if in prayer – the amazing praying mantis is actually a **(timid / fearsome)** hunter of the insect world. With lightning-fast speed, it uses its front legs to capture **(predators / prey)**. Sharp spikes on the forelegs **(help / supplement)** the mantis to hold insects tightly.

The praying mantis (also called the Mantis religiosa) eats all varieties of insects, **(excluding / including)** flies, grasshoppers, moths, caterpillars, beetles, and even bees. It is true that the female mantis will also sometimes **(marry / cannibalise / canonize)** their male partner! Meanwhile, they typically lay anywhere from 100 to 200 eggs at a time, which hatch in the spring. The mantis has an average life span of about one year.

The praying mantis has an **(odd / typical)** humanoid look – with two large compound eyes **(separate / set)** on a triangular head. The mantis can turn its head 180 degrees, allowing it to look behind itself. Some mantids **(create / design / develop)** wings, but they do not fly often.

The mantis can **(vary / disperse)** in size from one to six inches, and most are green or brown in appearance. Some are more colourful, and some have features that **(mimic / improve)** their environment, looking more like a stick or a dead leaf.

The praying mantis is not native to Great Britain, so it is **(likely / unlikely)** that you would **(endanger / encounter)** one in the wild. However, some have been occasionally spotted as they are bought as pets, or **(accidentally / primarily / intentionally)** imported from Europe with plants. Within Europe, the species has been **(importing | migrating / vacationing)** north in France, so perhaps in the coming years, they may be able to adapt to the environment in the south of England and **(contract / grow / spread)** further.

Select the best word from the choices of the underlined and highlighted words.

# Rio de Janeiro

Set against the **(backdrop / facade)** of mountains, a festive city and numerous beaches, Rio de Janeiro (or simply 'Rio') is a fantastic destination if you want to experience Brazilian culture. Rio de Janeiro – which means 'January River' – was named by early Portuguese **(natives / explorers)**. There is no river of that name in the city, so some people believe it was a **(mistake / error)**, others believe it was named after the month. At any rate, the name caught on and the city was founded in 1565 as part of the Portuguese **(embassy / empire)**. It remained under the control of Portugal until 1822, when it fought for its **(independence / subjugation)**. Rio became the capital of Brazil, although this was later moved to Brasilia.

Carnival is probably Rio's biggest **(distraction / attraction)**, for six days drawing over two million people onto the streets each day. Held before the **(observers / observance)** of Lent, Carnival has **(evolved / enhanced)** to be a giant celebration with parades, dancing, music, food and drink. Several exhibitions are organised featuring top **(dancers / actors)** from the local samba schools. There are also hundreds of informal street parties across the city.

Another **(iconic / ironic)** attraction of the city is a large statue of Jesus (called *Christ the Redeemer*) with outstretched arms, set on top of Corcovado Mountain. Measuring 30 metres tall, it sits on a 710 metres high **(peak / plateau)** and offers a spectacular view of the city and beaches.

The 2016 Summer Olympic Games were held in Rio, which marked the first time an Olympics had been held in **(North / South)** America. Brazil won seven gold medals during the games, **(their / there)** country's best results ever. (Interestingly, Great Britain finished second, with 67 medals.)

Rio has a **(topical / tropical)** climate, with the rainy season being between December and March. Temperatures can reach up to 40°C, but the averages fluctuate between 19°C and 30°C, making it perfect for a warm and sunny holiday.

# Call of the Wild

## (Jack London, 1903)

Buck did not read the newspapers, or he would have known that trouble was brewing, not alone for himself, but for every tide-water dog, strong of muscle and with warm, long hair, from Puget Sound to San Diego. Because men, groping in the Arctic darkness, had found a yellow metal, and because steamship and transportation companies were booming the find, thousands of men were rushing into the Northland. These men wanted dogs, and the dogs they wanted were heavy dogs, with strong muscles by which to toil, and furry coats to **expose** them from the frost.

Buck lived at a big house in the sun-kissed Santa Clara Valley. Judge Miller's place, it was called. It stood back from the road, half hidden among the trees, through which glimpses could be caught of the wide cool veranda that ran around its four sides. The house was **departed** by gravelled driveways which **straightened** about through wide-spreading lawns and under the interlacing boughs of tall poplars. At the **front** things were on even a more **poky** scale than at the front. There were great stables, where a dozen grooms and boys held forth, **columns** of vine-clad servants' cottages, an endless and **chaotic** array of outhouses, long grape arbors, green pastures, orchards, and berry patches. Then there was the pumping plant for the artesian well, and the big cement tank where Judge Miller's boys took their morning plunge and kept cool in the hot afternoon.

And over this great demesne Buck ruled. Here he was born, and here he had lived the four years of his life. It was true, there were other dogs. There could not but be other dogs on so vast a place, but they did not count.

They came and went, resided in the **deserted** kennels, or lived **clearly** in the **entrance** of the house after the fashion of Toots, the Japanese pug, or Ysabel, the Mexican hairless, strange creature that **usually** put nose out of doors or set foot to ground.

On the other hand, there were the fox terriers, a score of them at least, who yelped fearful promises at Toots and Ysabel looking out of the windows at them and protected by a legion of housemaids armed with brooms and mops. But Buck was neither house-dog nor kennel-dog. The whole realm was his.

He plunged into the swimming tank or went hunting with the Judge's sons; he **abandoned** Mollie and Alice, the Judge's daughters, on long twilight or early morning rambles; on wintry nights he lay at the Judge's feet before the roaring library fire; he carried the Judge's grandsons on his back, or rolled them in the grass, and guarded their footsteps through **tame** adventures down to the fountain in the stable yard, and even beyond, where the paddocks were, and the berry patches.

Among the terriers he stalked **meekly**, and Toots and Ysabel he **partially** ignored, for he was king -- king over all creeping, crawling, flying things of Judge Miller's place, humans included.

His father, Elmo, a huge St. Bernard, had been the Judge's **disconnected** companion, and Buck bid fair to follow in the way of his father. He was not so large— he weighed only one hundred and forty pounds—for his mother, Shep, had been a Scotch shepherd dog. Nevertheless, one hundred and forty pounds, to which was added the dignity that comes of good living and **limited** respect, enabled him to carry himself in right royal fashion.

Replace the highlighted words in the text below with the appropriate **antonyms** from the Word Bank. Use each word only once.

**Word Bank**: active, devoted, major, encouraged, contrasted, disobedience, tirelessly, aligning, organised, pacifists, conflict, extended, honoured, committed, peaceful

# Millicent Fawcett

Suffrage – the right to vote in elections – was not guaranteed for women in the United Kingdom until 1918. This important change was brought about by many **unfaithful** activists, working **briefly** for social change. Millicent Fawcett was one of these brave and **apathetic** campaigners.

Born Millicent Garrett, she was exposed to the cause of women's rights at a young age. While attending school in London, she supported the Kensington Society, which was a women's group **dispersed** to campaign for female suffrage. Meanwhile her sister, Elizabeth Garrett Anderson, became the first woman in Britain to ever qualify as a doctor in 1865.

In 1867 she married Henry Fawcett, a member of parliament and professor at Cambridge. He was also supporter of women's suffrage and **dissuaded** Millicent's involvement in the movement. In 1871 she helped to found Newnham House, which later became a women's college at Cambridge. After her husband died in 1884, she became even more politically active.

Fawcett became president of the National Union of Women's Suffrage Societies (NUWSS) in 1907, working to unite a coalition of campaigners who aimed at **violent** protest to gain their goals. This **conformed** with the Women's Social and Political Union (WSPU), led by Emmeline Pankhurst, who used civil **harmony**, hunger strikes and vandalism to affect change.

She eventually changed her mind about **separating** her efforts with a political party, after losing a vote for suffrage in 1912. The NUWSS then officially endorsed the Labour Party, as they were the only **insignificant** party that supported the right to vote for women.

When World War I began, Fawcett supported the country and the war effort, which put her against some of the other feminists who were **combatants**.

Support for women's suffrage had grown significantly during the war, as women had contributed greatly at home during the **peace**. Parliament finally granted the vote to women over the age of 30 in 1918, and in 1928 it was **closed** to all men and women over the age of 21.

Fawcett retired in 1919 after a lifetime of dedication to the cause of women's rights. In retirement she remained **sedentary** and wrote about her experiences. She was honoured for her service to the country with the Dame Grand Cross of the Order of the British Empire (GBE) in 1925.

In 2018, Dame Millicent Garrett Fawcett became the first woman to be **forgotten** with a statue in Parliament Square.

# JUST FOR FUN

## Animal Scramble

Unscramble the anagrams below to answer the questions about animals.

BOLSTER          FEARFIG          ROTRAP          GOROKANA

HIPLOND          RUGAJA           GARBED          ALOGLIR

MESHRAT          DOGHEEGH

1) Black and white striped creature that burrows under the ground.
_____

2) A small spiny creature found in woodland areas, meadows and gardens
_____

3) This is a crustacean you will find on the bottom of the sea
_____

4) This marine mammal is one of the most intelligent and can be found all over the world
_____

5) I have the longest neck!
_____

6) This large cat is not only dangerous, but an excellent swimmer
_____

7) A member of the rodent family that has become popular as a pet
_____

8) With it's strong hind legs, this creature can leap more than nine meters!
_____

9) A type of tropical bird with a strong, curved bill
_____

10) This giant herbivore has many human-like features and lives primarily in Africa
_____

# JUST FOR FUN
## W o r d L a d d e r s

Start from the word at the top of the ladder and work your way down to the bottom – by only changing just **one** letter from the previous word. You might also try to solve it from going from the bottom to the top! **Use the clues to help**.

Example:

HERE

HERD

HARD

CARD

CAT

1*

2*

DOG

1* clue: sultry or tropical
2* clue: pig

TRICK

1*

2*

CREED

3*

TREAT

FAIR

1*

2*

FOUL

1* Clue: do this on a boat
2* Clue: it's dirt

1* Clue: baby bird
2* Clue: the side of your face
3* Clue: it comes in loaves

106

PAPER

1*

TAKES

2*

COSTS

3*

CHAPS

4*

GLASS

£
£ £
£ £
£

NOISY

1*

PRISE

2*

CLIME

3*

4*

GUILE

5*

6*

QUIET

1* Clue: becomes narrower
2* Clue: luggage (plural)
3* Clue: outerwear (plural)
4* Clue: school group

1* Clue: self-composure, grace
2* Clue: examples are 2, 3, 5, 7
3* Clue: goo
4* Clue: shows you the way
5* Clue: regret, bad conscience
6* Clue: patchwork blanket

# Jumbled Sentences 1

Difficulty Level: Easy/Medium
(Suggested completion time: 20 minutes)

In these jumbled sentences, there has been a word added that **does** **not** belong. Select the word that does not belong from the choices given.

Example: umbrella because brought was gloves Glen his it raining

      A. brought
      B. gloves
      C. umbrella

*Answer: B*

1) did read novels not like criminal Isaac to crime

      A. criminal
      B. crime
      C. novels

2) new we the ridiculous a satisfying café lunch had in

      A. ridiculous
      B. satisfying
      C. café

3) unsafe the close tidy park council to the because it was decided

      A. unsafe
      B. close
      C. tidy

4) delivers any a parcel to moment Dad arrive at expecting was

      A. arrive
      B. delivers
      C. parcel

5) still Roman language that spoken Welsh in Wales is today is a

      A. Welsh
      B. spoken
      C. Roman

6) in the Severn United is the River longest estuary Kingdom the river

    A. estuary

    B. river

    C. the

7) quickly the man's settle calm helped to the stubborn nature disagreement

    A. calm

    B. settle

    C. stubborn

8) is chocolate indulgence favourite hot my moderation

    A. hot

    B. moderation

    C. indulgence

9) expensive Gerry an car will just sports bought

    A. expensive

    B. sports

    C. will

10) true in courage times the troops desperate showed rifles

    A. rifles

    B. desperate

    C. courage

    D. troops

11) sheer thunderstorm of hiking in a was shear madness idea the

    A. idea

    B. shear

    C. sheer

12) agreed both in principal to treaty principle the nations

    A. principal

    B. principle

    C. both

13) greatest  the  workers  asset  there  were  company's  their

      A. asset
      B. their
      C. there

14) inspect  the  pilot  hanger  the  aeroplane  went  to  his  in  hangar

      A. hangar
      B. hanger
      C. inspect

15) her  line  clothing  was  successful  new  launching  Gina  in  profits

      A. clothing
      B. profits
      C. successful

16) Nobel  the  physicist  imminent  Prize  won  eminent  the

      A. imminent
      B. Nobel
      C. eminent

17) the  lecture  interesting  Shakespeare  was  learning  on  professor's

      A. learning
      B. lecture
      C. interesting

18) made  a  purpose  to  Nico  London  journey  dangerous

      A. dangerous
      B. purpose
      C. journey

19) came  approximately  Freddie  home  6:00 p.m.  at  time

      A. came
      B. time
      C. approximately

# Jumbled Sentences 2

Difficulty Level: Medium/Hard
(Suggested completion time: 10 minutes)

In these jumbled sentences, there has been a word added that **does** **not** belong. Select the word that does not belong from the choices given.

1) soon   devastated   rains   unless   the   hydrated   will   be   it   crops

   A. devastated
   B. unless
   C. hydrated

2) gratifying   the   a   was   winning   experience   frustrating   competition

   A. frustrating
   B. gratifying
   C. winning

3) easily   his   make   unlike   Jules   did   not   complicated   friends   brother

   A. brother
   B. friends
   C. complicated

4) build   designate   to   had   Cedric   a   castle   plans   grandiose

   A. designate
   B. grandiose
   C. plans

5) the   wrong   made   organist   a   and   achievement   played   the   mistake   hymn

   A. mistake
   B. wrong
   C. achievement

6) amendments Alberto to any contract without debated agreed the

    A. amendments
    B. debated
    C. agreed

7) pandemic during the became fewer events in-person common less

    A. less
    B. fewer
    C. common

8) whom not meeting say with he met Martin would had

    A. meeting
    B. whom
    C. met

9) at job enjoyed her employed the Alice cinema part-time

    A. part-time
    B. job
    C. employed

10) leaders integrity we more with need integrated

    A. integrated
    B. integrity
    C. leaders

# Jumbled Sentences 3

### Difficulty Level: Medium
### (Suggested completion time: 10 minutes)

In these examples, try to find the word that is **missing**. Choose the word that is the best fit and would make a complete sentence.

Example: lessons   suggested   the   take   director   he

A. private
B. pirate
C. plenty

*Answer:* A

*The director suggested he take private lessons.*

1) into   ran   an   open   the   children

   A. grasses

   B. field

   C. green

2) his   doctor   to   it   university   become   was   and   a   attend

   A. attention

   B. desired

   C. ambition

3) grow   best   vegetables   soil   in

   A. dry

   B. fertile

   C. barren

4) the   clothing   designer   known   his   was   colourful   and   for

   A. flamboyant

   B. fragrant

   C. frequent

5) we to stay in a hotel had unfortunately

    A. delightful

    B. shabby

    C. dishevelled


6) an was after the emergency flooding

    A. distributed

    B. raining

    C. declared


7) boy and obstacle easily the was navigated the

    A. nimble

    B. liable

    C. clumsy


8) outside their the ability concentrate noise to loud

    A. effected

    B. affected

    C. assisted


9) had making a about her Mark do bad all the work

    A. conscience

    B. considerate

    C. condensation


10) wearing in was uniform always for school Henry his trouble

    A. correctly

    B. improperly

    C. illegibly

# Jumbled Sentences 4

Difficulty Level: Medium/Hard
(Suggested completion time: 10 minutes)

In these examples, try to find the word that is **missing**. Choose the word that is the best fit and would make a complete sentence.

1) cream  Mum's  strawberry  ice  favourite  is

    A. relaxing
    B. desert
    C. dessert

2) tonight  when  performing  we  will  don't  the  know  be

    A. band
    B. solo
    C. guitar

3) Snowdonia  our  by  climb  not  the  was  bad  of  weather  spoiled  to

    A. snow
    B. summit
    C. ruins

4) smartphone  has  location  a  that  Gemma's  shares  her

    A. feature
    B. complex
    C. aspect

5) choices  was  by  the  Davey  of  number

    A. bewildered
    B. controversy
    C. reached

6) Brian bottle a water always school to

    A. bought
    B. brought
    C. carry
    D. purchases

7) can a electrician finding challenging be

    A. sedentary
    B. unqualified
    C. best
    D. good

8) from I my email in Canada received cousin

    A. at
    B. an
    C. in
    D. above

9) the sells variety store a convenience sweets of

    A. selection
    B. extensive
    C. wide
    D. open

10) abandoned in mice seem the house the to

    A. hidden
    B. perished
    C. thrive
    D. adapting

# Jumbled Sentences 5

> The sentences below are in the incorrect order. Read through each and arrange them into the most logical order.

1) **A.** 'Not exactly,' answered Mum laughing.

   **B.** At breakfast, Mum announced that we would soon have a new family member.

   **C.** The day began with a big surprise.

   **D.** 'We're getting a kitten,' she said.

   **E.** 'You mean I'll have a new sister?' asked Annie.


2) **A.** But when she finally bought the headphones, all her friends wanted them too.

   **B.** She couldn't afford them, so she decided to get a part-time job.

   **C.** They did not understand why she was working so hard to save money.

   **D.** It was difficult, because her friends wanted to go out every weekend.

   **E.** Fiona saw an advertisement for some new wireless headphones.


3) **A.** 'None shall pass!' he shouted emphatically, surprising Reg and Dev.

   **B.** 'Good Sir,' Reg said to the giant, 'We must pass, for we are on a vital mission.'

   **C.** The ogre growled and rubbed his chin. 'What mission would that be?' he asked.

   **D.** The giant ogre looked down at the small creatures approaching.

   **E.** Startled, the two travellers looked up in fear, as they had never seen an ogre.


4) **A.** Relieved, he knew that everything would be all right.

   **B.** As a reward, his Dad let him borrow the car for the weekend.

   **C.** Suddenly, a pheasant appeared on the road, but he managed to stop in time.

   **D.** Joe had just passed his driving exam and had his new license.

   **E.** He decided that he would use the opportunity to visit his friend Alex.

5) **A.** There was a strange noise coming from outside.

   **B.** Surprised by the fox, Lydia called for her older brother to come downstairs.

   **C.** When her brother finally came down, there was nothing to see.

   **D.** She saw that a fox was in the back garden, trying to get into the bins.

   **E.** 'What happened?' her brother asked.

   **F.** 'There was a fox,' Lydia said, 'but he must have heard me and scurried away.'

   **G.** Lydia went to the window to see what was happening.

6) **A.** It's a long drive, but we can listen to music on the radio.

   **B.** For Easter, we usually go to my grandmother's house in the country.

   **C.** On the way back we listen to the old songs from the 80s that Mum likes.

   **D.** Grandma always has lots of sweets and cakes when we arrive.

7) **A.** Using her front paws, she boosted herself onto a chair to get a better look.

   **B.** The scent of chicken had attracted her attention.

   **C.** Then he looked down at the dog, who had a guilty look on her face.

   **D.** The hungry dog sniffed and looked up at the table.

   **E.** Knowing it was wrong, the dog leaned over and snatched the food.

   **F.** A boy walked into the room and asked, 'What happened to my sandwich?'

   **G.** She jumped down off the chair to finish eating it.

8) **A.** We realised it was a bank holiday and decided to go to the park instead.

   **B.** On the way, I met my friend Jaiden, who was also going to the High Street.

   **C.** We decided to go and shop together.

   **D.** I needed to go into town to get a new backpack.

   **E.** However, the stores were closed when we arrived.

# Analogies 1
### Difficulty Level: Easy
### (Suggested completion time: 10 minutes)

> Select the two words, one from each group, that will complete the sentence in the best way possible.
>
> *Example*:    **Tall** is to (short  medium  big) as **heavy** is to (tonne  boulder  light)
>
> Answer:    **short,  light**

1) **Kitten** is to (rabbit  cat  dog) as **foal** is to (elephant  fox  horse)

2) **Day** is to (spell  cloud  night) as **right** is to (flight  angle  left)

3) **Chapter** is to (library  learn  book) as **finger** is to (foot  hand  arm)

4) **Oar** is to (sail  swim  row) as **broom** is to (sweep  closet  kitchen)

5) **Study** is to (pencil  room  learning) as **exercise** is to (rest  fitness  illness)

6) **Surgeon** is to (cinema  house  hospital) as **porter** is to (hotel  restaurant  café)

7) **Oasis** is to (ocean  rainforest  desert) as **refuge** is to (park  storm  calm)

8) **Milk** is to (dessert  dairy  caramel) as **chicken** is to (feather  poultry  farmer)

9) **Remote** is to (control  promote  close) as **separate** is to (distract  leaves  together)

10) **Millennium** is to (10  100  1000) as **decade** is to (5  10  20)

11) **Hat** is to (hard  head  bowler) as **sock** is to (kick  wooly  foot)

12) **Apple** is to (melon  field  orchard) as **volume** is to (library  measure  container)

# Analogies 2
Difficulty Level: Medium
(Suggested completion time: 10 minutes)

Select the <u>two</u> words, one from each group, that will complete the sentence in the best way possible.

1) **Fear** is to (lonley  confidence  flight) as **sorrow** is to (happiness  anger  puppies)

2) **Wood** is to (forest  metal  paper) as **wool** is to (tree  sweater  shepherd)

3) **Wing** is to (laptop  aeroplane  submarine) as **tyre** is to (car  circus  river)

4) **Bread** is to (bun  slices  bakery) as **tea** is to (café  garage  cream)

5) **Rain** is to (quick  storm  sunshine) as **snow** is to (ice  blizzard  cloud)

6) **Elephant** is to (giant  pachyderm  jungle) as **leopard** is to (canine  feline  bovine)

7) **Benefit** is to (help  remove  loss) as **block** is to (chunk  obstruct  cube)

8) **Teacher** is to (desk  hide  classroom) as **conductor** is to (orchestra  plan  director)

9) **Dog** is to (paw  fur  tail) as **horse** is to (pony  hoof  stallion)

10) **Complete** is to (stack  whole  relief) as **beginning** is to (middle  origin  terminal)

11) **Atlas** is to (clothing  cups  maps) as **dictionary** is to (words  songs  recipes)

12) **Ice** is to (freeze  melt  drinks) as **steam** is to (engine  boil  dangerous)

# Analogies 3
Difficulty Level: Hard
(Suggested completion time: 10 minutes)

Select the <u>two</u> words, one from each group, that will complete the sentence in the best way possible.

1) **Mouse** is to (computer  rodent  cat) as **belt** is to (trousers  museum  shirt)

2) **Toad** is to (reptile  pond  amphibian) as **newspaper** is to (television  book  media)

3) **Letter** is to (words  write  envelope) as **oyster** is to (seafood  shell  ocean)

4) **Orange** is to (apple  yellow  fruit) as **carrot** is to (orange  vegetable  crunchy)

5) **Crane** is to (bird  construction  neck) as **chisel** is to (hammer  surgery  sculpture)

6) **Four** is to (five  for  quarter) as **pear** is to (green  shape  pair)

7) **Famine** is to (hunger  food  woman) as **arid** is to (man  density  water)

8) **Enemy** is to (state  foe  combatant) as **ally** is to (friend  join  peace)

9) **Loud** is to (scream  racket  music) as **quiet** is to (volume  speak  whisper)

10) **Coin** is to (pound  currency  round) as **paperback** is to (book  novel  publisher)

11) **Traitor** is to (personality  blazer  turncoat) as **jester** is to (laugh  wit  show)

12) **Contest** is to (prize  circle  oppose) as **grave** is to (dig  serious  cemetery)

# JUST FOR FUN
## RIver Crossing

Help Nancy get across the river to rescue her kitten. Going across, she can only step on the rocks with synonyms for 'ASSIST.' Coming back, she can only step on rocks containing a synonym for 'SAFETY'

Draw a line from rock to rock to help her find the right path.

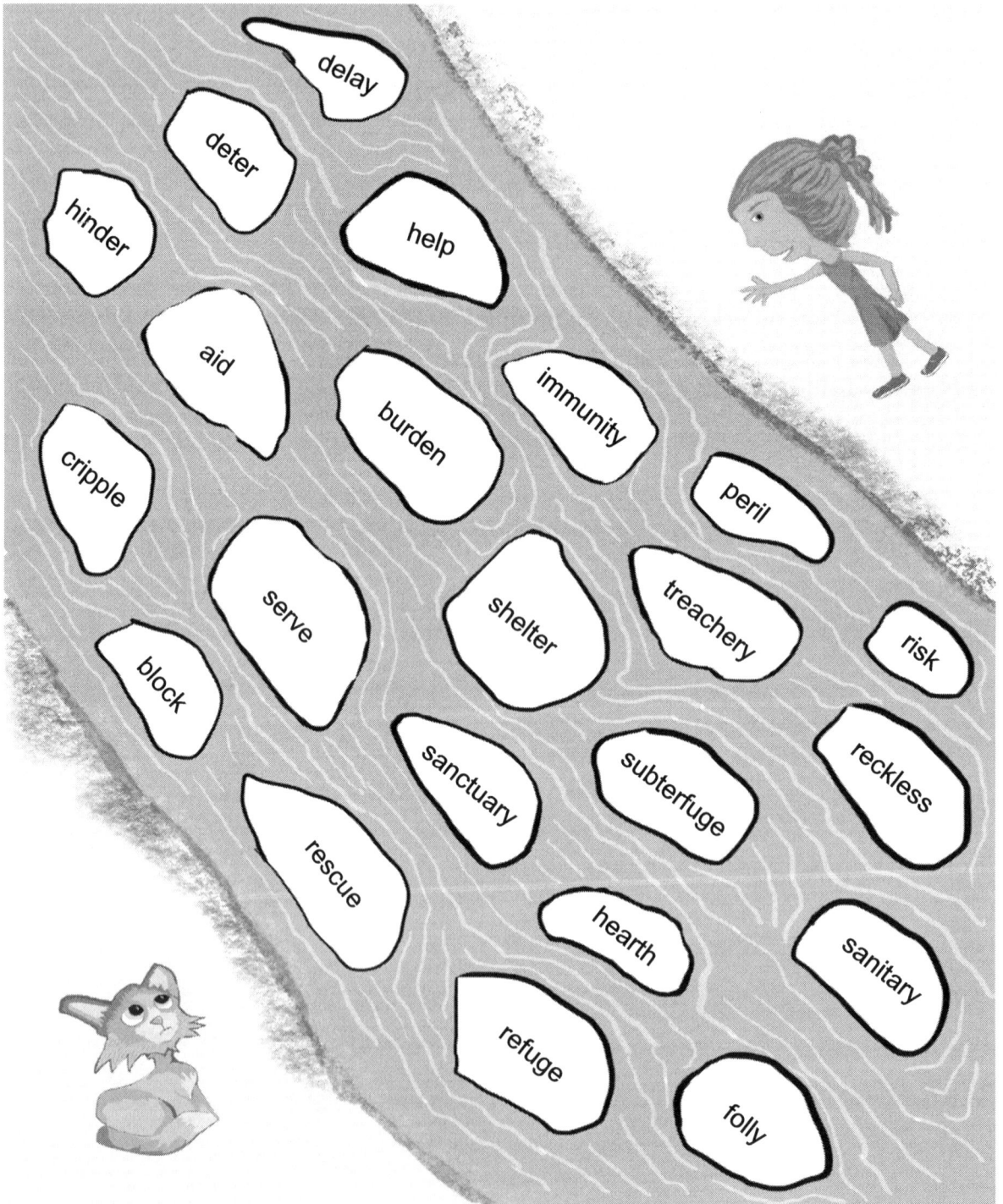

# What is True?

Difficulty Level: Medium/Hard

(Suggested completion time: 10 minutes)

In the questions below, read the sentences and then select the answer that is true, based on the given information.

1) John, Billy, Felicity and Emma are brothers and sisters.

   John is 3 years older than Billy.

   Felicity is older than John.

   Emma is 2 years younger than John.

   The ages of the children (not in order as given above) are 12, 10, 8, and 7.

   Which statement is true?

      a. Billy is older than Emma.

      b. Felicity is 12.

      c. Emma is the youngest.

      d. John is the oldest.

      e. The combined age of John and Billy is more than Emma and Felicity.

2) Fabian, Max, Beth and Mo live in London and like to travel to different countries.

   Fabian and Max have both been to France and Italy for school trips.

   Beth and Mo travelled to Spain and Portugal together last year.

   Mo is planning a trip to France and Belgium in the summer.

   Max went skiing in Austria two years ago.

   Fabian visited his grandparents in Denmark once.

   Beth used to live in Canada.

   Who has been to the fewest countries?

      a. Fabian

      b. Max

      c. Beth

      d. Mo

123

# Move a Letter

In this exercise, two new words can be formed by just moving **one** letter from the <u>first</u> <u>word</u>. The other letters **cannot** be changed, just the movement of the single letter to the second word as shown below. Select the letter and write down the two new words.

*Example*:  horse  tea

H  O  (R)  S  E

Answer:  hose, tear

Example:  bear  oat

(B)  E  A  R

Answer:  ear, boat

1)  alive  red

A  L  I  V  E

2)  flood  cap

F  L  O  O  D

3)  baker  are

B  A  K  E  R

4)  cause  fond

C  A  U  S  E

5)  peace  tap

P  E  A  C  E

6)  scale  ape

S  C  A  L  E

7)  first  tee

F  I  R  S  T

8)  though  edge

T  H  O  U  G  H

9)  dessert  elf

D  E  S  S  E  R  T

10)  launch  rely

L  A  U  N  C  H

11)  pirate  raid

P  I  R  A  T  E

12)  violent  arrow

V  I  O  L  E  N  T

# Rearranging Letters
Difficulty Level: Medium
(Suggested completion time: 10 minutes)

In this exercise, a new word is formed by rearranging letters from two different words. You will need to determine how the letters were changed with the first group and then change the letters in the same way in the second group of words.

Example:          (dog [log] lip)     (hat [ ? ] cob)
*The first letter of dog changes*

a. cat     b. hob     c. bat     d. hot

1)          (fact [fame] some)     (harm [ ? ] dock)
a. hick     b. hack     c. hark     d. dorm

2)          (tall [tale] joke)     (pace [ ? ] bolt)
a. bole     b. lace     c. pact     d. pale

3)          (held [have] gave)     (form [ ? ] wake)
a. worm     b. fork     c. fare     d. fake

4)          (pipe [pane] ants)     (then [ ? ] wise)
a. twin     b. with     c. when     d. seen

5)          (enemy [near] ratio)     (short [ ? ] empty)
a. shot     b. hemp     c. hope     d. home

6)          (fruit [ring] grown)     (found [ ? ] yodel)
a. node     b. food     c. only     d. lone

7)          (mouse [emit] write)     (phase [ ? ] thick)
a. pick     b. epic     c. hack     d. this

8)          (super [easy] abbey)     (booth [ ? ] ultra)
a. boot     b. rath     c. tuba     d. hoot

125

# Alphabet Code 1

In these questions, you will use the alphabet below to help answer the questions. Find how the letters are compared and then select the best answer.

*Example:*  **ST** is to **UV** as **FG** is to ?          Answer:  **HI**

ED    ( HI )    AB        GF

A B C D E F G H I J K L M N O P Q R S T U V W X Y Z

1) **AC** is to **EG** as **KM** is to ?

   a. OR    b. GI    c. PR    d. OQ

2) **BT** is to **CS** as **HZ** is to ?

   a. GY    b. IY    c. IZ    d. SY

3) **PR** is to **QU** as **GI** is to ?

   a. HL    b. HK    c. IM    d. HJ

4) **BC** is to **YX** as **FG**

   a. TS    b. WU    c. UT    d. VU

5) **AB** is to **CE** as **JK** is to ?

   a. LM    b. LN    c. MO    d. MN

6) **LM** is to **JN** as **UV** is to ?

   a. TW    b. TU    c. SW    d. SX

7) **AJ** is to **LM** as **KT** is to ?

   a. WX    b. UV    c. VX    d. VW

8) **TR** is to **GI** as **YW** is to ?

   a. BC    b. BD    c. AC    d. DF

# Alphabet Code 2

Difficulty Level: Medium/Hard
(Suggested completion time: 10 minutes)

In these questions, you will use the alphabet below to help answer the questions. Find the pair of letters that **fits the pattern** of the first four pairs.

*Example*:      AZ    BZ    CY    DY    [ ? ]              Answer:  **EX**

a. AZ    b. ZA    c. DX    d. EX    e. EY

A B C D E F G H I J K L M N O P Q R S T U V W X Y Z

1) AC    DD    EG    HH    IK    LL    [ ? ]
    a. MN    b. MO    c. AA    d. AA    e. MP

2) AC    BD    EG    FH    IK    [ ? ]
    a. LJ    b. JK    c. LN    d. JL    e. LO

3) GC    CE    MI    IK    TP    [ ? ]
    a. PR    b. PQ    c. RT    d. OQ    e. QR

4) WX    WT    RS    RO    MN    [ ? ]
    a. MI    b. MK    c. NJ    d. LI    e. MJ

5) BA    CD    JI    KL    RQ    [ ? ]
    a. TS    b. QS    c. ST    d. RQ    e. SV

6) EG    FI    GI    HK    IK    [ ? ]
    a. JL    b. JM    c. LN    d. MN    e. IM

7) BB    EE    II    NN    [ ? ]
    a. RR    b. SS    c. TT    d. UU    e. VV

8) AB    DE    HI    MN    [ ? ]
    a. PQ    b. QR    c. RS    d. TU    e. ST

# Alphabet Code 3

Difficulty Level: Medium/Hard

(Suggested completion time: 10 minutes)

---

In these questions, you will use the alphabet below to help answer the questions. Try to work out the code to get the right answer. (Note: Each question has a <u>different</u> code)

*Example*: If the code for **GLOVE** is **HMPWF**, what is the code for **HAND**?

a. GBOC    b. JCPF    c. GBOE    d. GZMC    e. IBOE

Answer:  **IBOE**

---

A B C D E F G H I J K L M N O P Q R S T U V W X Y Z

1) If the code for **RED** is **UHG**, what is the code for **STOP**?

a. VWRS    b. UVQR    c. WVQR    d. STOP    e. RTNQ

2) If the code for **ROBIN** is **NKXEJ**, what is the code for **MAGPIE**?

a. JXDMFB    b. HVBKDZ    c. IWCLEA    d. IXCLEA    e. IWDMDA

3) If the code for **LEMON** is **QJRTS**, what is the code for **ORANGE**?

a. UXGTMK    b. OWFSMJ    c. SVERKI    d. TWFTLJ    e. TWFSLJ

4) If the code for **CAR** is **AYP**, what does **ZSQ** mean?

a. SUB    b. BUS    c. TOP    d. BAR    e. BUT

5) If the code for **SMALL** is **CWKVV**, what does **QSKXD** mean?

a. BRAVE    b. GAUDY    c. GREAT    d. GIANT    e. LARGE

6) If the code for **TONE** is **OJIZ**, what does **WGDK** mean?

a. BLIP    b. SLIP    c. TRIP    d. FLIP    e. DROP

# The Tricky Spellings
## For Reference & Practice

In the Eleven Plus, excellence in spelling is important for numerous verbal reasoning type questions, such as various cloze exercises and anagrams. You may also find synonym and antonym questions that rely upon correct spelling knowledge.

As a teacher and eleven plus tutor, these are many of the most commonly misspelled words that I come across with children, year on year.

In many cases, mnemonic aids have been provided to help you remember the spelling or use of the words. The mnemonics used are focused upon the notoriously difficult parts of the word in question. You may already know some of these, but even adults still make mistakes with them!

**a lot** *pronoun* - a large number or amount; *adverb* - a great deal, much

The word 'alot' **does not exist!** Remember a lot is two separate words.

You *can't use* <u>alittle</u> so you ***don't use*** <u>alot</u>!

**allot** *verb* - to give something, divide by share, for a particular purpose; to designate or put aside

Remember there are two *l's* in allot.

I'm going to share these books with my children.

That's a lot to **allot**.

**absence** *noun* - not being present; not existing

absen**t** becomes absen**ce**

*James had a __c__ommon __e__xcuse for his absen__ce__ from school*

**accelerate** *verb* - make happen faster, to increase speed

*Two fast __c__ars (two __c__'s) in a__cc__elerate*

**accept** *verb* - agree to receive something; say yes to an invitation or offer; to consider something good or satisfactory

**except** *preposition, conjunction* - something not included; *verb* – specify as excluded from a group

These two words sound very similar

## **ac** + cept = accept

*Please accept this crazy carpet (acc)*

## **ex** + cept = except

*Nothing except extra care will save the planet (exc)*

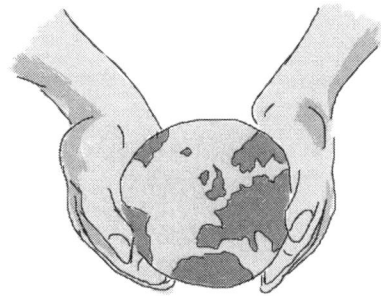

**accidentally** *adverb* - by chance or mistake

Two *c's* and two *l's* in accidentally

*A close and caring ally will help you in an accident*

**accommodate** *verb* - provide with a place to live; to fit in with the needs of someone or something; assist

**C    C**

**M    M**

*The accommodation had two Comfy Chairs and a Mega Mattress*

**accompany** *verb* - go with someone as a companion

Don't forget the two *c's*

You are good company C !

You too C !

COMPANY

**accurate** *adjective* - correct in all details, exact

Remember that **accurate** also has two *c's*

*Look twice to be certain.*
*See (**C**) it twice*

**acknowledge** *verb* - accept or admit the truth, or existence of something; to tell someone you have received something they sent

To acknowledge is to *KNOW*
ac**know**ledge

Did you bring any pizza?

I **know** you're on the **ledge**. That's why I brought the ladder!

**acquaintance** *noun* - someone you have met, but do not know well

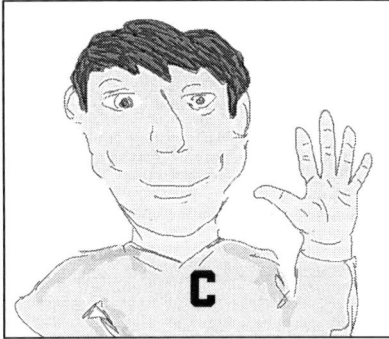

Focus on the **c** at the beginning

*You see ( **c** ) an a**c**quaintance from time to time*

**advice** *noun* - an opinion or recommendation offered to help you

*Advi**c**e is en**c**ouragement*

Don't confuse with advise

ADVI**C**E = noun
ADVI**S**E = verb

Advice: Free
Lemonade: £1

**aerial** *adjective* - happening in the air;  *noun* - a TV antenna

*It's not a**e**rial without an **E!***

*A**e**rial **E**ddie flies in loops*

Don't forget the *e*

| **affect** *verb* | **effect** *noun* |
|---|---|
| to make a difference to something | a change which is the result of an action |

**Affect = ACTION**

**Effect = Change**

# RAVEN =

**R**emember **A**ffect is a **V**erb, **E**ffect is a **N**oun

*use the raven to remember*

---

********** more on effect (use as a NOUN) **********

| An **effect** can also be an image or sound used in a play, television show or movie<br><br>*'The movie had some great special effects.'* | An **effect** can also be a personal item or belonging<br><br>*'Before departing the train you should make sure you haven't forgotten any personal effects.'* |
|---|---|

**aggressive** *adjective* - behaving in an intense, angry and possibly violent way; being forceful to get something or win

Don't forget that there are two g's and two s's in aggressive:

***Two** sides go to war –*
***G** and **S** want more*

134

**among** *preposition* - in the middle of, or surrounded by others; being included as part of a group

Among **(or also amongst)** is sometimes misspelled with a *u*

A **m_on_**(k) was a_mong_ them.

**analysis** *noun* - the process of studying something in detail

Why does my analysis always have a **Y**?

I don't know wh**y**, **Sis**

Remember there is a *y* where you might expect an *i* in analysis.

**anchor** *noun* - a heavy weight that keeps a boat from floating away; someone or something that gives support when needed

An an_chor_ is held by a **_ch_**ain **or** something else.

**ancient** *adjective* - of or from a very long time ago

<u>A</u>ncient <u>N</u>ames <u>C</u>an <u>I</u>nspire <u>E</u>very <u>N</u>ew <u>T</u>ale

**angle** *noun* - a measurement of the intersection of two lines

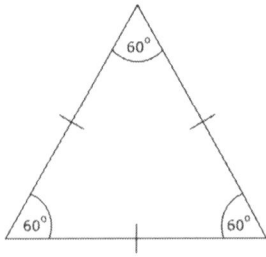

Don't confuse
angle with angel:

Angl**es** **L**ie **E**verywhere

The ang**el s**ang **el**egantly

**appearance** *noun* - when someone is seen in public; the way a thing or person looks to others

ap • **pear** • ance

**A p**ea and a **pear** made an **appea**rance

Hello!

**arithmetic** *noun* - Study of mathematics (addition/subtraction/ multiplication/ division)

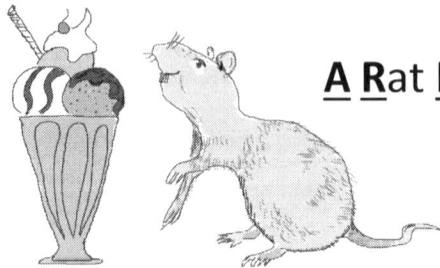

**A R**at **I**n **T**he **H**ouse **M**ay **E**at **T**he **I**ce **C**ream

**ascend** *verb* - to go up, or climb something; rise to a higher position

**descend** *verb* - to go down, or come down

It is easier to think about both words as they have similar spellings.

*Don't forget the C*

*Climbers **a**s**c**end, then **de**s**c**end the mountain*

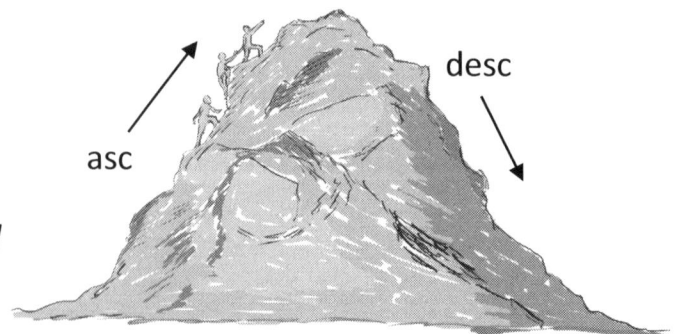

asc

desc

**assassination** *noun -* the murder of a prominent person

There are two sets of s's in assassination. You can use this phrase to keep that in mind:

*An assassination is **s**omething **s**erious and **s**ometimes **s**topped.*

Just stop it, Johnny!

**attached** *adjective -* joined, fastened or connected to something; full of affection

*The T's are a**tt**ached*

**autumn** *noun -* the season after summer and before winter

Key is not to forget the *n* at the end of the word.

**Think of <u>N</u>ovember at the end of autum<u>n</u>**

**awe** *noun -* a feeling of respect, wonder and fear

Remember the *e*...            ***A**lways **W**onderful and **E**xciting*

**awkward** *adjective* - difficult to deal with; causing problems, worry or embarrassment

*Two w's make this a**w**k**w**ard*

Another W and we could be on the web

Awkward!

**axis** *noun* - an imaginary line about which an object rotates; a fixed line on a graph used to show the position of a point

***Don't*** *put an e in axis!*

*I use lines, not an ax**e**, to make an axis*

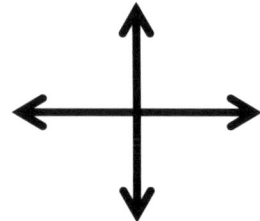

**bargain** *noun* - something at a lower price than its true value; an agreement made between two people or groups

*It's not a b**a**rg**a**in without two a's!*

The most common mistake is to forget the final *a*.

**basically** *adverb* - referring to the main or most important characteristic or feature

Try to remember there are two l's forming the word ***all*** after *basic*

*Basic**all**y you need them **ALL***

**beautiful** *adjective* - very attractive; pleasing to the senses or mind

Beau! You're beautiful!

Thanks.

***B**ig **E**lephants **A**re **U**sually <u>beau</u>tiful*

**because** *conjunction* - for the reason that

<u>*B*</u>*ig* <u>*e*</u>*lephants* <u>*c*</u>*an* <u>*a*</u>*lways* <u>*u*</u>*nderstand* <u>*s*</u>*mall* *elephants*

I know exactly what you mean.

**before** *preposition, conjunction, adverb* - prior to; in preparation for; in front of

*Don't forget the <u>e</u> befor<u>e</u> it's too late!*

befor e

**believe** *verb* - think that something is true or real

Amazingly, the word <u>lie</u> is placed in the middle of believe.

It cures all ailments!

SNAKE OIL

*Don't be<u>lie</u>ve a lie!*

ailment = illness

**bizarre** *adjective* - very strange and unusual; peculiar

Remember there is only one *z* and two *r*'s

*It is bizarre and **z**any that **a**ll **r**hinos **r**ead **e**verything*

What are you reading?

Shakespeare

**bruise** *noun* - an injury appearing as a discoloured mark on the skin; *verb* - to develop a bruise, or to cause someone to have a bruise

***B**rian **r**ubbed **U**ncle **I**an's **s**ore **e**lbow*

**business** *noun* - the activity of buying and selling goods or services; a particular company doing business; matters that relate to a person

There are three s's but no z in business

*There's a **bus in** every **s**uccess **s**tory*

**calendar** *noun* - a document that shows the days, weeks, and months of a year; a list of events and dates that are important to note

Try to remember that calendar ends with *-dar* not *-der*!

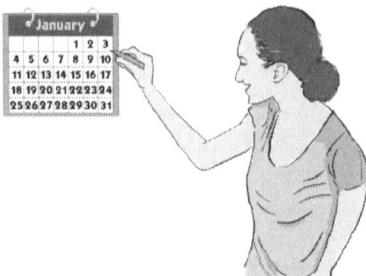

| January |
| 1 2 3 |
| 4 5 6 7 8 9 10 |
| 11 12 13 14 15 16 17 |
| 18 19 20 21 22 23 24 |
| 25 26 27 28 29 30 31 |

***Da**ra checked the calen**dar***

**careful** *adjective* - paying attention to avoid a mistake or accident

The common mistake is to add an extra *l* to make it *full*.

*Be **careful** **not** to make it **full***

In fact, for all adjectives, remember to spell the ending as **-ful** and not with two l's.

---

**category** *noun* - a class or division of things, or people regarded as having similar characteristics

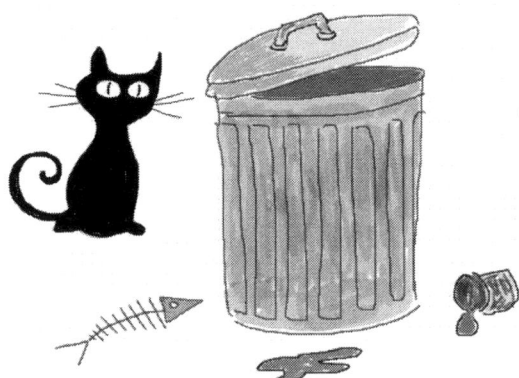

Remember the *e* in the middle

# The **cat** **e**ats **gory** stuff

(gory = gruesome, unpleasant)

---

**caught** *verb* - past tense of catch; took possession of something

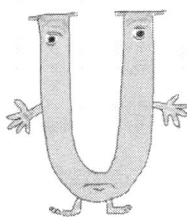

*You (**U**) are **cau**g**ht** between the **A**rmy and the **G**uards*

---

**ceiling** *noun* - the upper interior surface of a room; a top limit set on prices, wages, or spending; the maximum height an aircraft can reach

*See (**C**) the **e**levated **i**lluminations on the **cei**ling*

**cemetery** *noun* - a place where the dead are buried

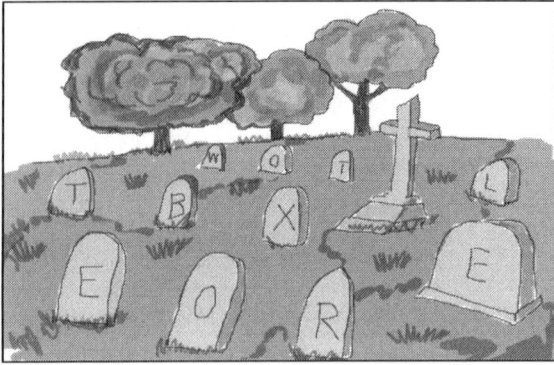

Remember there are **three e's** but **no a's** in *cemetery*

**or**

*E! E! E!*

*There are no a's in the cemetery*

*The ghosts say, 'E, E, E' (cemetery)*

**chaos** *noun* - complete disorder and confusion

**Cyclones, hurricanes and other storms**

**chauffeur** *noun* - a person hired to drive a car or vehicle

Remember there are two U's and two F's in chauffeur

*Chauffeurs drive fancy friends and you (u) too! (2 u's)*

**choir** *noun* - a group of people who sing together

Think of a choir of Chimpanzees and Orangutans.

**Ch**impanzees & **o**rangutans **i**n **r**hythm

**chose** *verb* - past tense of choose; has selected, made a choice

Drop an *o* from choose to get ch*o*se.

Charles *chose* the **c**oiled **hose**

Coiled = a connected series of spirals or loops

**collision** *noun* - an accident where two moving objects hit each other; a conflict between opposing ideas

Think of two *l*'s coming together

*Two Learners (LL) will co**ll**ide if not careful*

**column** *noun* - an upright pillar that usually supports a structure; a vertical division of a page or text

Here you need to remember the silent *n*.

*Think of a **ma n** on top of a tall colu**mn***

Is that you, Neil?

**committee** *noun* - a group appointed to represent a larger group of people to make decisions or collect information, research something

Try to remember the three sets of double letters (*m, t, e*) in committee:

*Two monkeys (**MM**), two tigers (**TT**), and two elephants (**EE**) were on the* **co<u>mm</u>i<u>tt</u>e<u>e</u>**

**compliment** *noun* - an expression of praise or admiration; *verb* - to praise or express admiration for someone

Well done! Bravo!

A **compl<u>i</u>ment** puts you in the **lime**light

**complement** *noun* - something that enhances, completes or improves another thing ; *verb* - enhance, complete or improve another thing

Butter compl<u>e</u>ments bread

A **compl<u>e</u>ment** <u>e</u>nhances

**concede** *verb* - to admit that something is true; to accept defeat; to give away something

Focus on the word *once*, which is hidden within:

*Only <u>C</u>oncede **ONCE** you have <u>D</u>one <u>E</u>verything*

**conscience** *noun* - a sense of personal belief in what is right and wrong, which guides ones behaviour and actions

Conveniently, if you remember how to spell science, then conscience should be somewhat easy:

*Use **SCIENCE**
when spelling **CONSCIENCE***

**correspond** *verb* - have a close similarity, match or be equal; to communicate by writing

Remember there are two *r's* in *correspond*:

*To co**rr**espond there must be two **r**eplies
(2-r's)*

**could** *verb*
past tense of can; used to ask permission; used to indicate a possibility

**should** *verb* used to describe what is correct, an obligation or duty; used to say what is probable

**would** *verb*
past tense of will; used to show a possibility, a request, willingness or desire

Oh, you lucky duck!

Must have won the lottery.

All three can be remembered using **OULD** – "**O**h **U** **L**ucky **D**uck"

**counterfeit** *noun* - an exact copy of something for usually dishonest purposes; *adjective* something made to appear genuine, with usually bad intent; *verb* imitate something fraudulently

The difficult part is the second *e* – showing up where it seems it should not. Try remembering the *-feit*:

*Counter**feit** –*
***F**akes **E**xposed **I**n **T**ime*

**courtesy** *noun* - polite behaviour or action

**Court • esy**
*He showed her a*
*courtesy on the*
**court**

Remember the *ou* in *court*

**crucial** *adjective* - of extreme importance; key to the success of something

***C**rucial **r**ules **u**pset **c**rocodiles **in a** l*agoon

Remember the *u* and *c* in crucial

NO SWIMMING

**cupboard** *noun* - a cabinet with doors used for storage

The difficult part is usually to remember the *p*

*Put the **CUP**s in the **cupboard***

**curiosity** *noun -* an interest to know or learn about something; something that is interesting because it is rare or unusual

There is a loss of the second *u* from the adjective *curious.*

I believe Bitcoin will come back this year

*Cats usually reach interesting opinions sitting in the yard*

* Never take investment advice from a cat

**deceased** *adjective -* dead

**dec • eased**
*In December the pain eased*

**deceive** *verb -* to hide the truth

Deceive does follow the 'i before e except after c' rule, but you also need to remember that there is an *ei* combination in *deceive:*

*Ellie's Intuition told her she was being deceived*

**definite** *adjective -* something that is certain; *noun -* something that is certain to happen

Remember there are two i's in definite

**de • fin • ite**

*I must think twice (two i's) to be definite*

**description** *noun* – a written or spoken statement about a person, thing or event, that tells you what it is like

Focus on the word is *script*:

de **script** ion

What did you think of my script?

It defies description

**desert** *noun* - a sandy area without much rain

**dessert** *noun* - a sweet dish served at the end of the main meal

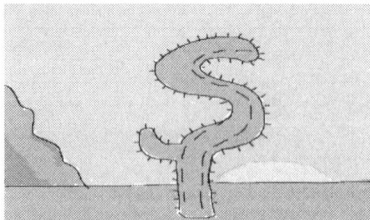

Desert or dessert? Keep these rules in mind:

*A desert is pretty empty – only one S*

*A dessert is Sweet Stuff – and plenty of it*

**destroy** *verb* - to damage something so that it cannot be used; completely defeat; ruin someone emotionally

The key to remember this spelling is to use an *e*

*Enemies destroy*

**difficulty** *noun* - a problem; not easy to understand or to do

Sometimes saying the letters aloud can be a good memory tip. Here is a phrase that may be helpful:

D I FFI C U LTY

(Say Aloud) 'Mrs. **D**, Mrs. **I**, Mrs. **FFI**, Mrs. **C**, Mrs. **U**, Mrs. **LTY**'

**disappointed** *adjective* - sad or upset because something did not happen that was wanted

Remember that there is only one *s* and two *p's* in *disappointed*

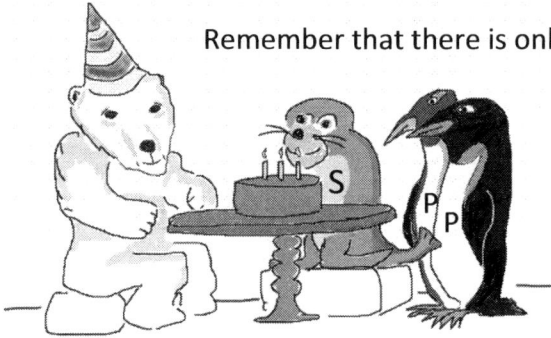

*Sally was disappointed that only **one Seal** and **two Penguins** could make it to her birthday party*

**disastrous** *adjective* - extremely bad; causing great damage

In the adjective disastrous there is a missing *e* from the noun *disaster*.

*The day turned disastrous when the Emu escaped **(no e)***

**discipline** *noun* - the ability to control yourself according to strict rules; a particular area of study, especially at a university

Think of the word disc to help remember the correct spelling.

*The **disc I p**layed was on the **line***

**discuss** *verb* - talk about a subject with someone

Remember there are two s's in discuss

*He discussed the **disc** with **U**ma, **S**teve, and **S**am*

**doubt** *noun* - a feeling of uncertainty, or hesitation; *verb* - feel uncertain about something

*Be (**b**) in dou**b**t*

Which ones are the Marigolds?

Don't forget the **b**
in dou__b__t

*The **b**ee was in **doubt** about which flowers he liked, and those he did not*

---

**dreamt** *verb* - past tense of dream; have experienced dreams

This spelling is included because it is the only word in English that ends in -*mt*.

<u>*Dreams and **m**ore*</u>
<u>***t**rances (MT)*</u>

---

**Egypt** *noun* - a country in Northern Africa

*__E__very __G__oat __Y__ells '__P__arty __T__ime!'
in Egypt*

**eight** *number* - the number 8

*<u>E</u>ight <u>I</u>s <u>G</u>reat - <u>H</u>ope you can <u>T</u>olerate (so many legs!)*

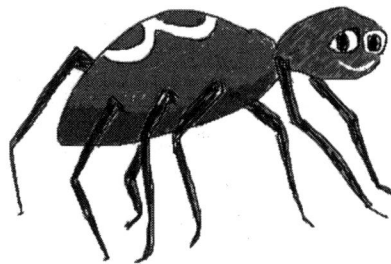

**embarrass** *verb* - cause someone to feel self-conscious, nervous, or uncomfortable

Remember the two *r's* and two *s's* in *emba<u>rr</u>a<u>ss</u>*:

*Do you get <u>R</u>eally <u>R</u>ed <u>A</u>nd <u>S</u>mile <u>S</u>hyly?*

**emphasis** *noun* - a special importance to something in speaking or writing

*The <u>em</u>peror <u>ph</u>oned <u>a</u> <u>sis</u>ter*

Here we want to remember to use the *ph* for the *f*-sound, and the *a* for the *uh*-sound.

**environment** *noun* - the air, water, and land in and on which people or animals live

*or*

*An <u>IRON</u> can help in any envi<u>ron</u>ment*

<u>IRON</u> <u>MEN</u> *Train in any envi<u>ron</u>ment*

**equipped** *adjective* - having the necessary items for a task

Here it is good to remember that this word has two *p's*:

*It is important to be **equipped** for a **p**articular **p**urpose*

Did you remember the popcorn?

**essential** *adjective* - extremely important; *noun* a thing that is extremely important

The two *s's* are the key – or shall we say, **essential**?

*S̲turdy s̲ails are es̲s̲ential*

**exaggerate** *verb* - represent something as larger, more important, better or worse than it actually is

Remember that beside the two *g's*, the *-ate* ending.

First, I had the Basmati, then the Pilau, but the long-grain rice was my favourite

*The **g**igantic **g**iraffe liked to exaggerate about what he **ate***

**excellent** *adjective* - outstanding, superb

Remember there are two *l's* .
Think of the word cell:

*The ex**cell**ent wizard sat in his **cell.***

**existence** *noun* - the state of being real; a way of life

Keep in mind there are three *e's* in exist<u>e</u>nce:

*<u>E</u>veryone's*
*<u>E</u>xist<u>e</u>nce is*
*<u>E</u>ssential*

**extremely** *adverb* - very

Don't forget the final *e*

*Extrem<u>e</u> + ly*

***Extreme <u>e</u>lephants are extrem<u>e</u>ly rare***

**faithfully** *adverb* - in a loyal manner; in a factual or true way

This is a word where we do need the two l's in full.

*Every year Santa faith<u>fully</u> ensures the stockings are **<u>full</u>** of presents*

**familiar** *adjective* - well known because of having met, seen or heard before; in a close relationship

Try to remember there is only one *l*, by using the word *liar* that ends the spelling of familiar:

That **liar** looks fami<u>liar</u>

I don't be<u>lie</u>ve him

SNAKE OIL

**fascinate** *verb* - attract the attention and strong interest of someone

The key to spelling fascinate is to remember the *sc* combination, similar to science:

*Are you fa**sc**inated with **sc**ience?*

**February** *noun* - the second month of the year

feb • ru • ary
*<u>F</u>rosts, <u>e</u>ven <u>b</u>lizzards
<u>r</u>each <u>us</u> <u>a</u>nd <u>r</u>un <u>y</u>early*

**fiery** *adjective* - having a bright red colour; burning strongly and brightly; showing very strong feelings; spicy (food)

This would be an easier word to spell if the *r* and *e* were not reversing positions from *fire*.

*<u>E</u>ating <u>R</u>ed chilies can be fi<u>er</u>y*

**foreign** *adjective* - belonging to or from a country not your own; strange and unfamiliar, not belonging to something

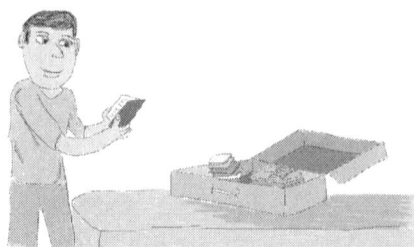

Here is another exception to the 'i before e' rule. Focus on the beginning of the word by using this aid with *before*:

*Be<u>fore</u> <u>I</u> <u>g</u>o to foreign <u>n</u>ations, I always check my passport*

154

**forty** *number* - the number 40

Remember to drop the *u* from *four* when going to forty

### You (*u*) forget when you're 40

How many candles, Mama?

---

**generally** *adverb* - usually, most of the time; broadly speaking

Try and focus on the two *l*'s by thinking of the word rally:

### *The general liked going to the* __*rally*__

---

**giraffe** *noun* - a tall mammal with a patterned coat and a long neck

*Two long-necked ff's make a giraffe*

# gira*ff*e

---

**government** *noun* - the people with authority to make laws and policies of a country, or region; the system of making and applying laws

Wear this instead, Your Majesty

### To **govern me<u>a</u>nt** removing the A and not forgetting the two N's

**grammar** *noun* - the system of rules and structure of a language

Remember the two *m's* as well as to end with *ar* and <u>not</u> er.

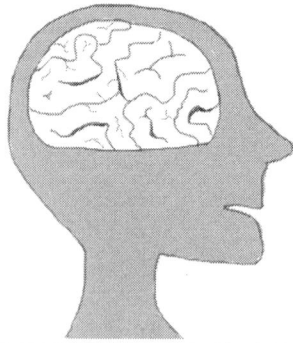

*You don't have to be a* **m**a*ster***m**i*nd to go **far** with good gramm**ar***

**guarantee** *noun* - a formal promise; a warranty; *verb* make a formal assurance of certain conditions; to promise with certainty

Remember both the -ua and two e's

*The **guar**dian **an**t **tee**s off*

**handkerchief** *noun* - a small square cloth used for wiping the nose or eyes

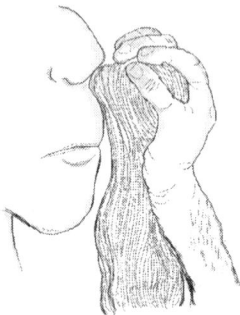

Remember the d in *handkerchief*.

*Use your **hand** to hold the <u>hand</u>kerchief*

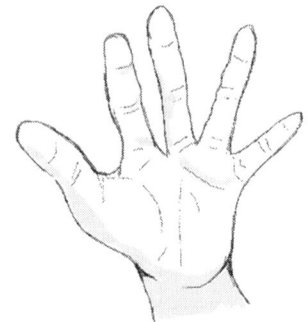

**hangar** *noun* – a building used for storing aircraft

**hanger** *noun* - a shaped frame for storing clothing

A hang<u>a</u>r is used for <u>a</u>eroplanes

A hang<u>e</u>r is used for <u>e</u>veryday clothes

**harass** *verb* - annoy or upset someone

Bullies!

Remember the single *r* and two *s's*

*The double S har**ass**ed the single R*

**height** *noun* - the distance from the top to the bottom of something; the distance of something measured above a surface

**weight** *noun* - the heaviness of something expressed as a measure; an object that is heavy

Try to remember these together as they are both measurements and have the word *eight* contained within:

*The **height** and **weight** total **eight**!*

**H + W = 8**

**heroes** *noun* - (plural of hero) someone who is admired for their bravery or their achievements

*<u>E</u>xplorers and <u>S</u>portspeople are some of our hero<u>es</u>*

*Hero<u>es</u> are <u>e</u>xtra <u>sp</u>ecial*

**humorous** *adjective* - funny

*You (<u>u</u>) are humoro<u>us</u> only at the end*

The *u* changes position from humo<u>ur</u> to humoro<u>us</u>:

*It was humoro<u>us</u> to <u>us</u>*

**independent** *adjective* - not influenced or controlled by an outside authority; not taking any financial or other assistance

The trick is to remember the three *e's*

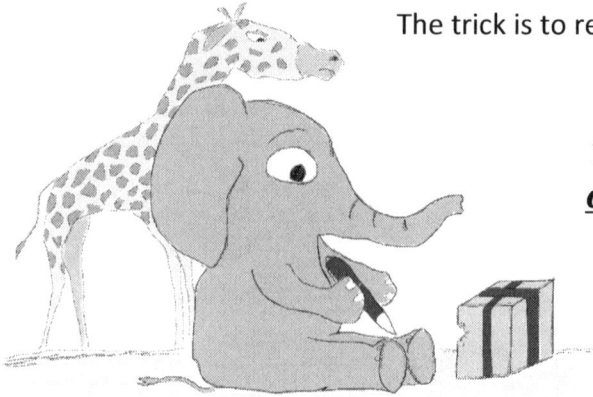

*The **e**lephant's **pen** made a **dent** in the giraffe's present*

**innocent** *adjective* - not guilty of a crime; not responsible or involved in an event; *noun* - a pure or naïve person

***In no cent**ury is murder innocent*

**intelligent** *adjective* - clever, smart

$\sqrt{5xy}$

***In tell**ing, the **gent** showed he was **intelligent***

**interrupt** *verb* - stop the progress of a conversation, activity, or process for a short period

*It is **r**eally **r**ude to inte**rr**upt*

Remember there are two *r's* in interrupt:

**irritable** *adjective* - easily annoyed

Don't forget the two *r's*

*Arrgh! (**R**) Missing an **R** is ir**r**itable*

**jewellery** *noun* - decorative items that are worn, such as necklaces, rings, and bracelets

Don't forget the two *e's and two l's*

***Elle** really loves jew**ell**ery*

**language** *noun* - a communications system of speaking and writing

***U** (you) should really learn a lang**uag**e at your **age***

**laugh** *noun* - a sound made to show you are happy or have found something funny

***L**augh **a**nd you'll (**u**) **g**et **h**appy!*

**league** *noun* - a group of teams playing a particular sport, who compete with each other; a group of people or countries who join together for a specific purpose

*The Premier League*
*lets eager adults get unusually*
*excited*

**leisure** *noun* - time when you are not working; the use of free time to do things that are enjoyable

*Lions eat immense steaks*
*at leisure*

**length** *noun* - the measurement of an object from one end to the other; the amount of time something lasts

Don't forget the *g*

*Increase the length with G*

**liaise** *verb* - cooperate with another group on a subject of mutual concern; to act as a link between two different groups or people

Try to remember the two *i*'s on either side of the *a*:

*Isabelle and Ivy*
*must liaise*

**library** *noun* - a building or room containing a collection of books, periodicals, and other materials, for use by the public or members

Remember the two *r's* by focusing on *rar*:

*You can find **rar**e books in the lib**rar**y*

**lightning** *noun* - the natural electrical discharge between a cloud and the ground, usually with a bright flash of light during a storm

Don't put an *e* in lightning!

*Everyone escaped from the lightning (no E)*

**loose** *adjective* - not tight or firmly fastened in place

**lose** *verb* - no longer have something; be defeated in a competition

Think of the m**oo**se, which sounds like l**oo**se (or goose)

Lose and loose are sometimes misspelled because of the o.

*The m**oo**se is l**oo**se!*

*Only one **o** in l**o**se*

**maintenance** *noun* - the process or work required to keep something in good condition; financial support for someone's living expenses

*The **main** work was done by **ten** ants (**ance**)*

**manoeuvre** *noun* - a movement that requires skill to complete; a military exercise; *verb* - move carefully or guide something

That's quite the manoeuvre!

*Standing a **man** **o**n **e**very **u**mbrella (is a) **v**ery **r**are **e**vent*

**marvellous** *adjective* - amazing, extraordinary

Remember to use two *l's*

*ladybirds and leopards have marvellous spots*

**meagre** *adjective* - a very small amount that is not enough

Meagre is spelled with *-re* like agree

*Me agrees – that's meagre*

**medallion** *noun* - a metal disc worn on a chain or string around the neck; a small round cut of meat with no bones

*They gave the **medal** to the **lion***

162

**medieval** *adjective* - relating to the Middle Ages (approx. AD 600 – 1500)

Next time, don't eat all the cookies!

*Medi**eval** people may have been brutal, but that didn't make them evil*

Remember the *-val* ending instead of *–vil*
Also keep in mind the word *die* in the middle of me*die*val

**millennium** *noun* - one thousand years

*1000 years last **l**ong and **n**eed **n**umbering*

There are two *l's* and two *n's* in *millennium*

1    250         500         750         1000

**miniature** *adjective* - describing a small copy of something; *noun* - a very small copy of something

*There's a **mini** '**a**' hidden in the minia̲ture town*

*(can you find it?)*

**minimum** *noun* - the smallest amount necessary or possible; *adjective* - describing the smallest amount required or possible

*To keep mistakes to a minimum, I like to take my **Mini Mum** with me from time to time.*

Don't forget your homework!

**mischievous** *adjective* - describing behaviour that causes trouble but is not meant to be harmful

*__Mis__erable __Ch__arles __i__nserted __e__xtra __v__egetables __on__ __us__*

**muscle** *noun* - tissue in a human or animal body that can contract, in order to produce movement

Focus on the *CL* in muscle

*__cl__imbing improves mus__cl__es*

**naïve** *adjective* - showing lack of experience, wisdom or judgement; too willing to believe someone is telling the truth; innocent

*__A__rtificial __I__ntelligence can be n__aï__ve sometimes*

Where are my fingernails?

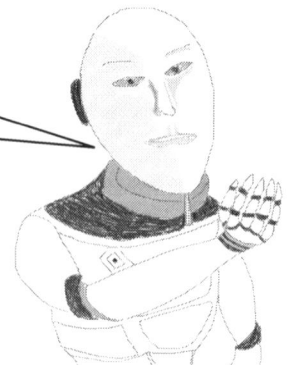

Note: The double dot over the *i* in naïve is called a **diaeresis**. This means the *a* and *i* have their own separate sounds

**necessary** *adjective* - needed for a particular purpose

THE **NECESSARY** BRAND
COMFORTABLE • SIMPLE • STYLISH

*It is ne__cess__ary for a shirt have one __c__ollar and two __s__leeves*

**niece** *noun* - a daughter of one's brother or sister, or a daughter of one's wife/husband's brother or sister

*My **n**iece **is e**xtremely **c**areful with **e**lephants*

**noticeable** *adjective* - easily seen, or recognised

You forgot the E!

*It is notic**e**able if you forget the **E***

**novel** *noun* - a long written story with imaginary characters or events; *adjective* - new or unusual

***N**ovels **o**ffer **v**ery **e**xciting **l**anguage*

Action
Sci-Fi
Adventure
Thriller

**occasion** *noun* - referring to a particular time or event; a special event; *verb* - to cause something

*For a special o**cc**asion – travel over two seas (two **c**'s)*

How many seas have we seen?

Two on this o**cc**asion

c c

**occur** *verb* - happen; exist

*See (**C**) it occurs twice!*

C          C

**parallel** *adjective* - lines that are side by side and have the same distance between them

## para · ll · el

*Parallel* has **parallel lines** in the middle and one *l* at the end

**parliament** *noun* - a group of people who are elected to make laws for a country

Remember the *i* in the middle of parliament
by focusing on *I am*

*I **am** in the parl**iam**ent*

**piece** *noun* - a portion, or section of something; an artistic creation; *verb* - assemble something from parts

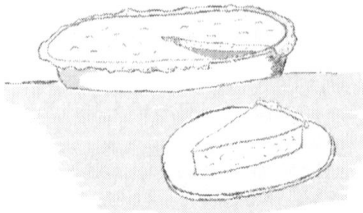

**peace** *noun* - calm and quiet; a period of time without war

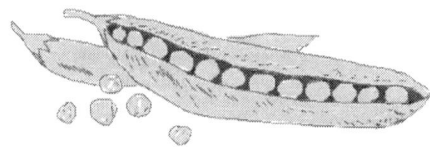

A **pie**ce of **pie**

Give **pea**s (peace) a chance

**people** *noun* - collective term for humans; members of a particular country or group

How about sharing some of your oranges?

*People* *eat* *oranges*, *people* *like* *eating*

**permanent** *adjective* - intended to last indefinitely; *noun* - a type of hair treatment that lasts for a few weeks

The horse's **mane** was per**mane**nt

I'm not changing my style for anyone

**perseverance** *noun* - determination to finish a job or achieve a goal despite difficulty and hardship

They've been at it for hours!

That's some perseverance!

*Pers*ons *ever* (at the) d*ance*

**persuade** *verb* - convince someone to do something by using reason or argument

Remember the u in the middle

JOB INTERVIEWS →

*You (**u**) must persuade them*

**pharaoh** *noun* - a ruler in ancient Egypt

*P̲lease h̲ear a̲bout r̲ulers*
*a̲nd o̲ther h̲eroes*

**pigeon** *noun* - type of bird with a small head and typically grey and white feathers

Remember there is no 'd' in pigeon

*The p̲ig̲eon saw a **pig** e̲ntering*

**poison** *noun* - a substance that causes severe illness or death; *verb* - to give poison to someone or an animal

PHARMACY

Do you have any Hemlock?

*The **Po**(tion) **is on***
*the list*

potion = a liquid
with special abilities

**possession** *noun* - the fact of having, owning or controlling something; an article or something that is owned

Remember the four s's in po̲ss̲ess̲ion

*S̲ilver S̲wans and S̲apphire S̲tones –*
*that's a lot of po̲ss̲es̲sions!*

**practice** *noun* - exercise repeated to gain or improve a skill; a habit or custom; a job or business that requires a lot of training and skill

**practise** *verb* - perform an activity regularly in order to gain or improve skills; carry out an activity on a regular basis

Think of *ice*:

*The nurse put **ice** on it in the doctor's pract**ice***

Ends in *ise*:

*Prac**tise** **to** **i**mprove **s**ports **e**xcellence*

**pray** *verb* - to speak to a god or another deity to express love, thanks or to ask for something

**prey** *noun* - an animal that is hunted and killed for food by another animal

***A**ngels pr**ay***

***E**agles pr**ey***

**principal** *adjective* - the most important, main; *noun* - the most important person in an organization

**principle** *noun* an idea or belief that is the basis for making decisions or a system of belief; a scientific theory

*The prin**ce** is not your **pal***

principle

rule

*princip**le** ends with **le** just like ru**le**.*

169

**prise** *verb* - use force to take something apart, away or open something

**prize** *noun* - something given for winning a competition, or for a special achievement

He pri**s**ed open the can with the **s**crewdriver

The **Z**ombie won the pri**z**e

**pronunciation** *noun* how a word sounds when spoken

It's easy to spell pro**nun**ciation when you think of the nun

*The **nun** has good pro**nun**ciation*

**quay** *noun* - area where goods are loaded onto ships

Quay begins with *qu-* but sounds like *key*

*Join the **qu**eue tod**ay** to get the key*

**queue** *noun* - a line of people, waiting to enter, be served, or to buy something; *verb* - wait in a queue

***Q**ueens **u**sually **e**at **u**p **e**verything (as they don't have to **queue**).*

What are we waiting for?

*Also, imagine u's and e's lining up*

**reign** *verb* - rule as a monarch (King, Queen, Emperor, etc.);
*noun* - the period of rule of a monarch

**_R_**oyals **_e_**njoy **_i_**nviting **_g_**reat
(k)**_n_**ights

---

**restaurant** *noun* - a place where you can sit down and pay for a meal

*I'll **rest _a_**nd you (**_u_**) **rant***

Why don't you have Marshmallow pie? And what about Prune juice? I need to have some options... This is ridiculous!

rant = talk loudly or angrily at length about something

---

**rhyme** *verb* use words that have a same last syllable sound; *noun* - a word that has a same last sounding syllable as another word; a poem

Remember that the *hy* has the same sound as in the word *why:*

Having a ball, sitting here on the wall

Let's run away to a lovely little cafe We'll laugh all day Come what may

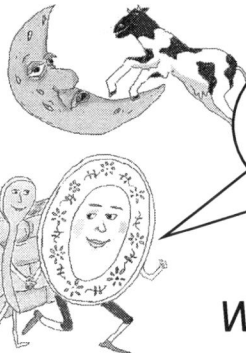

*W**_hy_** r**_hy_**me all the time?*

---

**rhythm** *noun* - a strong pattern of sounds or movement repeated in music, poetry or dance; the pattern of change or movements in nature

**_R_**hythm **_h_**elps **_y_**our **_t_**wo **_h_**ips **_m_**ove

**roofs** *noun* - (plural of roof) the top covering of a building or other structure housing people

*I've got to get that fixed soon.*

*The **r**oofs **o**n **o**ld **f**lats **s**ag.*

**sandal** *noun* - a type of open shoe held together with straps

***S**am **and Al**ice wore sandals*

Only <u>one</u> *l* in *sanda<u>l</u>*

**scene** *noun* - a place where something has happened or happens in a story, or in real life; a segment of a story, movie or play

Seen and scene sound the same, but remember the additional *c* and the re-ordering of the other letters

*The **S**ea **C**aptain **e**ats **n**achos **e**nthusiastically*

**schedule** *noun* - a timetable of events; *verb* - arrange or plan an event; include something in a timetable of events

*As a r**ule**, I sch**edu**le my afternoons at **sch**ool with the m**ule***

**scissors** *noun* - a tool used for cutting paper and other materials

Try to remember the middle *s's* in scissors

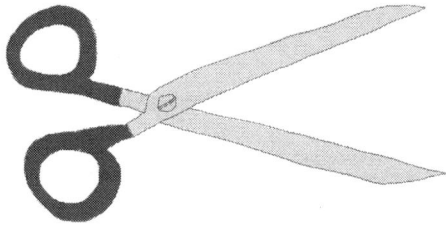

*S̲cissors c̲ut i̲n s̲imple s̲lices*

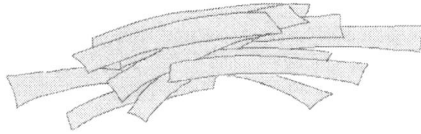

**seize** *verb* - grab, take hold of something

Focus on the *-ize* ending:

*Emma sei̲z̲ed the pri̲z̲e*

**separate** *adjective* - different, distinct; *verb* - move apart, divide

Remember to **separate** the two *a's*:

**or**

A̲ndy and A̲lex must be sep**a̲r̲a̲**ted

There's **a̲ r̲a̲t̲** in sep**a̲r̲a̲**te

**shear** *verb* - cut wool off a sheep (or hair off another animal)

**sheer** *adjective* - nothing but (provides emphasis); very steep; material that is almost see-through

sh**ee**r is for **e**xtra **e**mphasis

*'He made top grades through* **sheer** *determination'*

*'It was* **sheer** *coincidence that we met in London.'*

Don't sh**ear** the **ear**

**siege** *noun* - an attack using military forces to take a city or fortress

***S**oldiers **i**nvaded **e**very **g**round **e**verywhere*

**skilful** *adjective* - possessing skill, talented

Remember to drop one *l* from the word *skill*:

*Be skilful as you separate the two **l**'s*

**special** *adjective* - exceptional, outstanding; specific to a person or place; *noun* - a programme for television or broadcast for a particular occasion

*The Spe**cia**l Agent was from the **CIA***

CIA = Central Intelligence Agency (American agency that collects secret information)

**stationery** *noun* - paper, envelopes and writing instruments used to write letters or cards

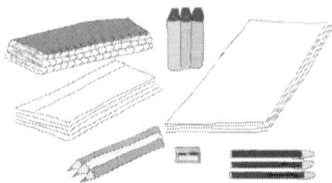

**stationary** *adjective* - fixed in one position, not moving

*STATION**E**RY and **e**nvelopes are **e**ffective for writing letters*

*STATION**A**RY is an **A**djective STATION**A**RY is **A**lways there*

**stomach** *noun* - an organ in the body where food is digested

*<u>Ch</u>eese gives me stom<u>ach</u> <u>ach</u>es*

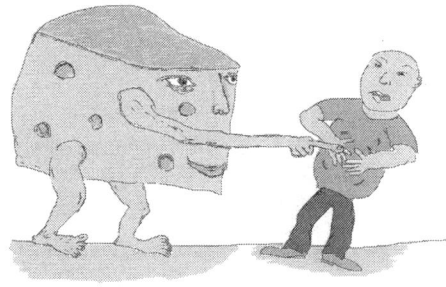

**subtle** *adjective* - not obvious, small but important; done in an indirect or tactful way in order to achieve something

Remember the *b* is silent

*Be (**B**) su<u>b</u>tle – it's quiet*

**success** *noun* the achievement of a goal or aim; a victory

Remember the two *c's* and two *s's*

*<u>C</u>ourage in <u>c</u>limbing <u>s</u>pells <u>s</u>u<u>cc</u>e<u>ss</u>*

**sufficient** *adjective* - enough

What **if**... we doubled the ***i's*** and the ***f's***?

*Double the **f**'s and **i**'s to be su<u>ffi</u>c<u>i</u>ent*

**suggest** *verb* - propose an idea; indicate or show something

Don't forget the two *g's* in suggest:

## *G*irl *g*uides make good su*gg*estions

**symbol** *noun* - a sign or letter used to represent something; a person or thing that represents or stands for something else

  1          2          3          4          5          6

## A symbol is a *s*ign *y*ou *m*ake *b*ased *o*n *l*anguage

   $\$$

  7          8          9          10

*Can you identify these symbols?*
*(See page 209 for the answers)*

**thorough** *adjective* – detailed and careful; complete; done with great care

That's every nail hammered! What's next?

## ***Thor*** *was* ***rough*** *and* ***thorough***

**tomorrow** *noun* - the day after today; *adverb* - on the day after today

Remember the double *r* like in bo**rr**ow and a**rr**ow

Are you ready for tomorrow?

Yes, but I might need some more arrows

*Tomo**rr**ow **r**equires **r**eadiness*

**tongue** *noun* - the organ in the mouth used to taste , swallow and help in speaking; a way or style of speaking

*A **tong** of good smells help you (**u**) **e**at*

**truly** *adverb* - honestly; accurately or correctly

Think of spelling July – no *e's*!

*It is tr**uly** hot in J**uly***

**twelfth** *number* - the 12<sup>th</sup> in a sequence

Twelve changes to tw**elf**th – use the elf to remember!

Who's next? Number twelve!

*The **elf** came after the 11th*

**twentieth** *number* - the 20<sup>th</sup> in a sequence

The *ty* in twenty changes to *tie* in twentieth

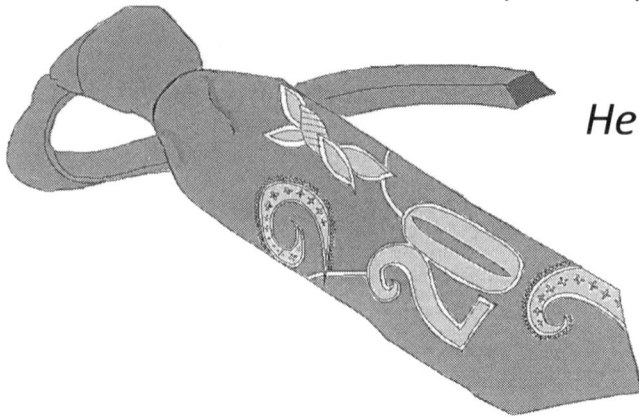

*He wore a **tie** to his twen**tie**th birthday*

**tyranny** *noun* - oppressive government rule; a situation where there is an unfair use of power

Two y's and two n's in tyranny

***T**rust **y**our **Granny**, not a **tyranny***

**unique** *adjective* - one of a kind

Are we there yet?

***Uni**nterest**ing **que**stions are not unique*

**unusual** *adjective* - not common, abnormal, surprising

Remember there are three *u's* in unusual

*It is **un**u**s**u**al to see you (**u**)
three times in one day*

**vacuum** *noun* - an electrical appliance that cleans floors and surfaces by using suction; a space without gas or matter

Remember there are
two *u's* in vacuum:

*Make sure you vac**uu**m **u**nder the **u**pholstery*

**vehicle** *noun* - a machine used to transport people and other items, usually over land; a medium used to express an idea

Don't forget the *h* in vehicle:

Your car has **hic**-ups!

HIC HIC

What's wrong with my ve**hic**le?

**vicious** *adjective* - showing a desire to be cruel or physically violent

Don't forget there is a *c* in vicious

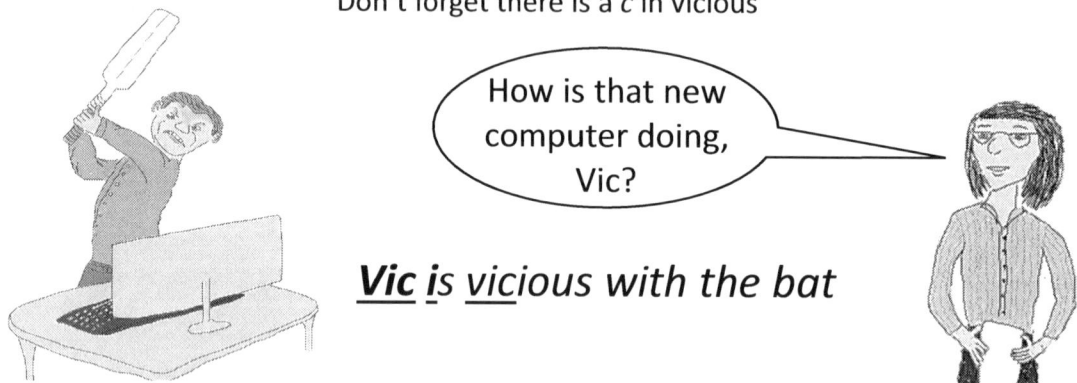

How is that new computer doing, Vic?

**Vic is** vi**c**ious with the bat

**weather** *noun* - the climate in terms of temperature, wind, rain, etc.; *verb* – change by exposure to the climate; successfully deal with a problem

**whether** *conjunction* - if; indicating a choice of alternatives

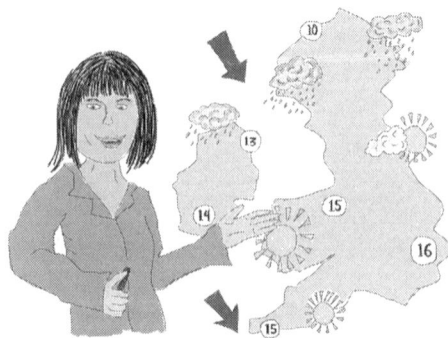

**We** (look) **at her** –
look at the **weather** lady

**W**hether **he t**ells **her** – that
is the question

**weird** *adjective* - strange; unnatural

<u>W</u>acky <u>e</u>lephants <u>i</u>n <u>r</u>ed <u>d</u>resses

Wacky = funny, or amusing in a strange way

**yacht** *noun* - a medium-sized boat used for racing or recreation

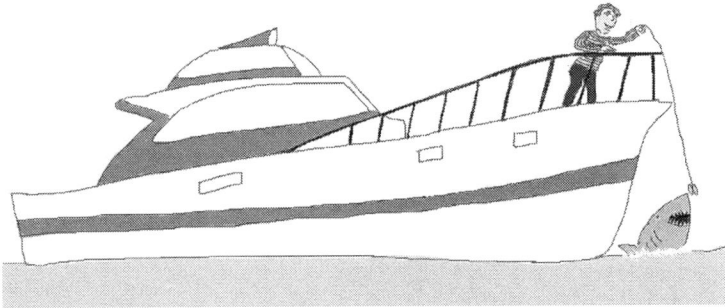

<u>Y</u>o-yos <u>a</u>re <u>c</u>ool, <u>h</u>andy, <u>t</u>oys to play on a <u>yacht</u>

# Spelling Test 1
Difficulty Level: Medium
(Suggested completion time: 10 minutes)

Choose the correct answer from the choices presented.

1) We had trouble finding **(there / their)** missing kitten in the neighbourhood.

2) Charlie did not know **(weather / whether)** he should stay or go home

3) If Mary couldn't play, then the team was sure to **(lose / loose)**.

4) Because Len doesn't like to go outside, he bought a **(stationery / stationary)** bike.

5) Tom lived by the **(principal / principle)** that you should treat everyone with respect.

6) Muriel's endless complaining had no **(affect / effect)** on me.

7) The highlight of Jim's summer was when his father **(sheared / sheered)** the sheep.

8) After ten years of hard work, Paula **(ascended / descended)** to the position of manager.

9) Belinda had an instinctive **(flair / flare)** for music.

10) **(There / Their)** are not many people as brave as my grandfather.

11) Jenny tried to **(prise / prize)** the ball away from the dog but she could not do so very easily.

12) I was too **(weak / week)** to put the case on the top shelf.

13) **(Accept / Except)** for Thurman, none of us knew how to speak Spanish.

14) The rain **(affected / effected)** our plans to go to the park.

15) Greg was bothered by a **(lose / loose)** tooth.

16) The rabbit **(prayed / preyed)** it would not get eaten by the wolf.

17) She always stored her dresses in the wardrobe on **(hangars / hangers)**.

18) The **(principal / principle)** reason we stayed was that we couldn't afford to go anywhere else.

19) Sometimes it is dangerous to walk outside in your **(bear / bare)** feet.

20) I could not **(accept / except)** such a generous offer.

# Spelling Test 2
Difficulty Level: Medium
(Suggested completion time: 8 minutes)

Fill in the missing letters in each sentence.

1) We tried our best to **a** ☐☐ **o** ☐☐ **odate** our visitors with the spare room.

2) Dell found it **a** ☐ **k** ☐☐ **rd** to have dinner with Fiona's parents.

3) December is the **tw** ☐☐☐ **th** month of the year.

4) My mother had to do annual **main** ☐☐☐☐ **nce** on the boiler.

5) Joe was **d** ☐☐☐☐ **pointed** that we didn't want to watch the Queen's speech.

6) We like to go to the orchard for fresh apples in the **aut** ☐☐☐ .

7) Paula told us a **humo** ☐☐☐ **s** story about the time she found a stray kitten in her handbag.

8) Jamie's trip to Spain was his first to a **fo** ☐☐☐ **gn** country.

9) The only bird we saw at the park was a hungry **pi** ☐☐☐ **n**.

10) I can **g** ☐☐☐☐ **ntee** that there will be another opportunity for success.

# Spelling Test 3

Difficulty Level: Medium
(Suggested completion time: 8 minutes)

Fill in the missing letters in each sentence.

1) The weather caused delays, cancellations and **c**[ ][ ][ ]**s** at the airport.

2) We bought matching rings at the **jew**[ ][ ][ ][ ]**ry** store.

3) During the **r**[ ][ ][ ]**n** of Elizabeth I, the Spanish Armada was defeated.

4) The bald eagle is a **s**[ ][ ][ ]**ol** of the United States of America.

5) *Robinson Crusoe* is a **n**[ ][ ][ ]**l** about a man's adventures on a desert island.

6) Rudi received a **comp**[ ][ ][ ][ ]**nt** for his choice of attire.

7) Tess would always **int**[ ][ ][ ][ ]**pt** when we were having a private conversation.

8) We **faith**[ ][ ][ ][ ]**y** feed the stray cat every evening.

9) Twelve vehicles were involved in the motorway **col**[ ][ ][ ]**ion**.

10) There are some **an**[ ][ ][ ]**nt** ruins near my cousin's farm in Italy.

# Spelling Test 4
Difficulty Level: Medium
(Suggested completion time: 8 minutes)

Fill in the missing letters in each sentence.

1) The ☐☐☐**ial** acrobatics were amazing at the International Air Tattoo.

2) Too much water and fertiliser can **d**☐☐☐**roy** your garden.

3) The **com**☐**i**☐☐☐**e** decided to use the extra funding to build a new library.

4) Clive used a **han**☐☐☐☐**chief** to clean off the windscreen.

5) Billy received a **min**☐☐☐☐**re** tool set in his Christmas cracker.

6) Margo ☐**c**☐**ld**☐**nt**☐☐☐**y** spilt ink all over the table.

7) There was a long **q**☐☐☐**e** outside the cinema.

8) Muriel ☐☐☐☐**pted** the gift graciously.

9) Jason doesn't like to use the **va**☐☐☐**m** because it is too noisy.

10) It is **gene**☐☐☐☐**y** a bad idea to handle a cactus with bare hands.

185

# Spelling Test 5

Difficulty Level: Medium

(Suggested completion time: 8 minutes)

Fill in the missing letters in each sentence.

1) Charles Dickens and Charles Darwin were both born in **F**☐☐☐☐**ary**.

2) There is a **marv**☐☐☐☐**us** new Indian restaurant open on the High Street.

3) Will you **a**☐☐☐**mpany** me in the garden?

4) My **misch**☐☐☐**ous** little sister took all the chocolate cake again.

5) Tim's **stom**☐☐☐ bothered him after eating too much for dinner.

6) Recycling is beneficial for the **envir**☐☐**m**☐☐**t**.

7) The average ☐☐☐**ght** of a male polar bear is 450 kilograms.

8) Julie found it hard to **be**☐☐☐**ve** that her brother was going to appear on a TV reality show.

9) The beauty of the seaside at sunset was beyond **desc**☐☐☐☐**ion**.

10) There was no **d**☐☐☐**t** that the sun would rise in the morning.

# Spelling Test 6

Difficulty Level: Medium

(Suggested completion time: 8 minutes)

Fill in the missing letters in each sentence.

1) Nigel **dr**☐☐☐**t** that he was a famous musician who toured the world.

2) We went to see Derrick's boat at the **q**☐☐**y**.

3) My teacher gave me some good **ad**☐☐☐**e** on how to handle pressure during the exams.

4) The archaeologist went to **E**☐☐☐**t** to participate in an important excavation near the pyramids.

5) I was surprised to hear that solar eclipses **o**☐☐☐**r** every 18 months.

6) Having a peacock appearing suddenly in your garden is **un**☐☐**u**☐**l**.

7) Maria's prize **pos**☐☐☐☐**ion** is a watch that was once owned by her great-grandfather.

8) Dad is usually **i**☐☐☐**table** when he must take the car to the garage.

9) The bank warned that we should be aware of **counterf**☐☐☐ pound notes.

10) Trinity's ☐**b**☐**en**☐**e** was felt strongly by her friends.

# Spelling Test 7
Difficulty Level: Medium
(Suggested completion time: 8 minutes)

Fill in the missing letters in each sentence.

1) I fell on the ice and got a bad **br**☐☐**se** on my right hip.

2) John thought he lacked the **dis**☐☐**pli**☐☐ to be a better athlete.

3) The flies would always **ha**☐☐☐**s** the cattle in the field.

4) Elena tried to **p**☐**rs**☐**ad**☐ her parents to buy the latest iPhone for her sixteenth birthday.

5) Iris has a reputation as the club's most **ski**☐☐☐**l** chess player.

6) It was a difficult **mano**☐☐**v**☐☐, but Sally managed to drive out of the crowded car park without any problems.

7) Li won the award for best performance in her age **cat**☐**g**☐☐**y**.

8) Be **extr**☐**m**☐☐**y** careful when lighting a campfire.

9) We had to **la**☐☐**h** when Theo bought engine oil instead of olive oil for the salad.

10) The change in her appearance was **notic**☐☐**bl**☐ after she was appointed headmaster.

# Spelling Test 8

Difficulty Level: Medium

(Suggested completion time: 8 minutes)

Fill in the missing letters in each sentence.

1) Kim worked out in the gym four times a week to improve his **mus**☐☐☐ tone.

2) In their new house, Joe and Ben have **sep**☐**r**☐**t**☐ bedrooms.

3) He was an **a**☐☐**uaint**☐**nce** from school, but not a close friend.

4) Some of the headstones in the **c**☐**m**☐**t**☐**ry** date back to the 1700s.

5) In his **l**☐☐**sure** time, Luke enjoys writing and performing electronic music.

6) On this **o**☐☐**as**☐**on**, we decided to take the train to London.

7) Monica had to check her **ca**☐☐**nd**☐**r** to see if she was free to attend the concert.

8) Mum sometimes uses **s**☐☐☐**sors** to cut the pizza.

9) I had to give my room a **th**☐☐**o**☐☐**h** cleaning.

10) Freddie had to **a**☐☐**now**☐☐**dge** defeat in his attempt to swim the English Channel.

# Palindrome Fun

Palindromes are words or phrases that can be spelt the same way backwards (right to left) as normally. Here are some of the more common single word palindromes:

| | | | |
|---|---|---|---|
| **CIVIC** | **DAD** | **EVE** | **GAG** |
| **GIG** | **KAYAK** | **LEVEL** | **LOL** |
| **MADAM** | **PEEP** | **RACECAR** | **RADAR** |
| **REFER** | **ROTATOR** | **ROTOR** | **SOLOS** |
| **STATS** | **TENET** | **TOOT** | **WOW** |

Palindromes get even more interesting when they are extended to phrases or complete sentences. Here are some particularly funny and interesting ones.

Never odd or even

**evil olive**

senile felines

gold log

**taco cat**

Top spot!

A nut for a jar of tuna.

Step on no pets.

No, it is opposition.

Was it a car or a cat I saw?

**Neil, an alien.**

Dee saw a seed.

Rise to vote, sir.

## Mr. Owl ate my metal worm!

Name now one man.

Ed is on no side.

Madam, I'm Adam.

No lemons, no melon.

Panda had nap.

Nurses run.

Emil saw a slime.

No, it is opposition.

## Borrow or rob?

Must sell at tallest sum.

Yawn a more Roman way.

A man, a plan, a canal – Panama

Are we not drawn onward to new era?

Marge lets Norah see Sharon's telegram.

Anne, I vote more cars race Rome to Vienna.

I madam, I made radio! So, I dared. Am I mad? Am I?

## Cigar? Toss it in a can. It is so tragic.

# Answer Key

**Synonym Pairs 1, Page 7**

1) amount, measure  2) company, business  3) harbour, quay  4) foe, enemy  5) sly, crafty
6) brief, short  7) guarantee, promise  8) deadly, fatal  9) obvious, apparent  10) mercy,
forgiveness  11) sphere, orb  12) catastrophe, disaster  13) elegant, stylish  14) beverage,
drink  15) original, authentic

**Synonym Pairs 2, Page 8**

1) hoax, trick  2) clever, bright  3) curb, restrain  4) profit, gain  5) depart, exit  6) charming,
sweet  7) abundant, plenty  8) refuse, deny  9) honourable, distinguished  10) fatigue,
weariness  11) flat, level  12) hollow, void  13) acquire, obtain  14) admission, revelation
15) branch, limb

**Synonym Pairs 3, Page 9**

1) employ, engage  2) excavate, dig  3) clear, apparent  4) embellish, decorate  5) futile,
hopeless  6) severe, harsh  7) nonchalant, casual  8) chaos, disarray  9) summit, peak
10) unpredictable, erratic  11) contrary, opposite  12) brief, concise  13) sleek, shiny
14) vacant, empty  15) tumult, uproar

**Synonym Pairs 4, Page 10**

1) ambition, desire  2) heist, theft  3) jester, wit  4) pioneer, innovator  5) bountiful, abundant
6) indulge, pamper  7) temporary, brief  8) precise, exact  9) restore, remedy  10) wise,
astute  11) diminish, decrease  12) vain, conceited  13) vast, extensive  14) crucial, critical
15) perish, die

**Synonym Matching, Page 11**

1) variety – assortment,  2) section – slice,  3) resemble - mirror, 4) excitement – hysteria,
5) link – connection,  6) scour – scrub,  7) burst – rupture,  8) tremendous – massive,
9) generic – common,  10) veer – swerve,  11) progress – advance,  12) agree - accept

**Just for Fun – Spiral Puzzle, Page 12**

1) Aqueduct,  2) Torrent,  3) Tide,  4) Eel,  5) Lake,  6) Evaporation,  7) Navy,  8) Yacht,
9) Turtle,  10) Erosion, 11) Nautical,  12) Lemonade

**Antonym Pairs 1, Page 13**

1) unite, divide  2) plunge, rise  3) scarce, plentiful  4) flee, arrive  5) valid, false  6) praise, blame  7) neglect, care  8) optimistic, gloomy  9) eager, disinterested  10) sincere, deceitful  11) core, minor  12) scatter, assemble  13) necessary, non-essential  14) embarrassed, confident  15) obvious, unclear

**Antonym Pairs 2, Page 14**

1) grow, decline  2) boastful, modest  3) healthy, sick  4) discourage, promote  5) generous, miserly  6) bold, timid  7) reluctant, keen  8) strict, lenient  9) fleeting, enduring  10) mayhem, calm  11) adequate, insufficient  12) danger, safety  13) typical, unusual  14) allow, object  15) ascend, drop

**Antonym Pairs 3, Page 15**

1) skilful, awkward  2) obnoxious, pleasant  3) cacophony, silence  4) youthful, elderly  5) ancient,  modern  6) confined, liberated  7) deliberate, accidental  8) novice, expert  9) contradict, agree  10) natural, artificial  11) detach, affix  12) unkempt, tidy  13) vague, distinct  14) stationary, mobile  15) confuse, clarify

**Antonym Pairs 4, Page 16**

1) blunt, dull  2) assist, discourage  3) constant, variable  4) acknowledge, deny  5) stubborn, flexible  6) fatigue, energy  7) respectful, impolite  8) destitute, affluent  9) feasible, impossible  10) effortless, arduous  11) sage, unintelligent  12) vigilant, careless  13) permit, obstruct  14) akin, unrelated  15) impeccable, flawed

**Antonym Matching, Page 17**

1)  reluctant – enthusiastic,  2) frivolous – practical,  3) retain – discard,  4) conquer – lose,  5) spontaneous – calculated,  6) flourish – wither,  7)  ignore – obey,  8) deception – honesty,  9) required – unnecessary,  10) arctic – tropical,  11) curt – polite,  12) vigilant – careless

## Synonyms Word Blocks 1, Pages 18-19

1) ROBUST – Strong,  2) EXPAND – Swell,  3) INFERIOR – Lesser,  4) ADEPT – Capable,

5) EMPTY – Vacant,  6) BURDEN – Load,  7) SURPLUS – Excess,  8) SOLE – Lone,

9) ADEPT – Nimble,  10) ASSIGN – Designate,  11) AVOID – Dodge,  12) MEET – Contact,

13) FLOATS – Buoyant,  14) ATTRACTIVE – Pretty,  15) CAPTIVATING – Riveting,

16) ABSURD – Ludicrous,  17) HOME – Habitat,  18) NEEDED – Required

## Synonyms Word Blocks 2, Page 20

1) CANCEL - Abandon,   2) LUCRATIVE – Profitable,  3) OBEDIENT – Compliant,  4) DISTRESS –

Torment,  5) CHORTLE – Laugh,  6) FATHOM – Comprehend,  7) ELUSIVE – Slippery,

8) SAFE – Sheltered,  9) VENERABLE – Esteemed,  10) INTERFERE – Intrude

## Synonyms Word Blocks 3, Page 21

1) TEDIOUS – Boring,  2) VIVACIOUS – Lively,  3) SURPASS – Exceed,  4) DISTORT – Twist,  5)

SOMBRE – Serious,  6) NONCHALANT – Casual,  7) ABHOR – Detest,  8) JEOPARDY – Danger,  9)

BLUNDER – Mistake,  10) UNHURRIED – Slow

## Antonyms Word Blocks 1, Pages 22-23

1) DOUBT – Trust,  2) DISPUTE – Agree,  3) DISMAL – Bright,  4) GENUINE – Fake, 5) HAMPER –

Help,  6) RARE – Common,  7) GENTLE – Severe,  8) FINISH – Embark, 9) DETACH – Join,

10) ENDLESS – Limited,  11) CONTENT – Worried,  12) DIMINISH – Grow,  13) DIFFERENT –

Identical,  14) FRAGILE – Sturdy,  15) IGNORE – Heed,  16) AFFLUENT – Poor,  17) CORDIAL –

Hostile,  18) YOUNG – Elderly

## Antonyms Word Blocks 2, Page 24

1) FICKLE – Constant,  2) BROKEN – Intact,  3) HASTE – Delay,  4) DORMANT – Awake,

5) STINGY – Generous,  6) NUISANCE – Help,  7) VAGUE – Clear,  8) THWART – Assist,

9) ORDEAL – Calm,  10) ORIGIN – End

## Antonyms Word Blocks 3, Page 25

1) ANCIENT – Recent,  2) GULLIBLE – Suspicious,  3) FAIR – Biased,  4) RUTHLESS – Gentle,

5) UNITY – Division,  6) SPEND – Save,  7) CRAMPED – Spacious,  8) PETITE – Large,

9) SLOW - Rapid  10) APEX – Bottom

**Crossword 1 (Antonyms), Pages 26-27**

ACROSS:  3) WAIT, 6) SURVIVE, 7) ONCE, 10) SCATTER, 12) VOLUNTARY, 15) LAG, 18) RANDOM, 21) REMAIN, 22) OVERT, 23) COY, 24) QUALITY

DOWN:  1) BEST,  2) SHRINK, 3) WRECK, 4) THAW, 5) SILENCE, 8) READY, 9) TRIVIAL, 11) SOLUTION, 13) TAIL, 14) ROUGH, 16) AGAINST, 17) COURTEOUS, 18) REJOICE,  19) OMIT, 20) DEFY

**Crossword 2 (Antonyms), Pages 28-29**

ACROSS: 1) DETAIN, 4) ARID, 6) BOILS, 7) STRONG, 9) SOON, 10) PECULIAR, 12) TAKE, 13) DECEIT, 14) ANTI, 16) COWARDICE, 19) NAY, 21) BENT, 22) REJECT, 23) OPAQUE, 24) TENSE, 27) CATCH, 29) ROT, 30) EGO, 31) CEASE, 32) SEA, 33) GRIEVE, 34) IGNITE, 35) CYNIC

DOWN: 1) DISSUADE, 2) NEGLECT, 3) VOWEL, 4) ASSERTIVE, 5) DIN, 8) RELIC, 11) SEPARATE, 15) TRANSFORM, 16) CONCEALS, 17) ATTRACT, 18) LENIENT, 20) BROAD, 25) EMERGE,  26) ERECT, 27) CONVEY, 28) HOAX, 30) EPIC

**Crossword 3, Pages 30-31**

Across:

1) humble, 3) tease, 8) mound, 9) local, 10) flop, 11) demolish, 13) angel, 14) frequently, 18) dab, 19) equal, 20) victory, 22) sly, 23) death, 25) bizarre, 27) rodents, 29) neigh, 30) typical

Down:

1) halt, 2) expand, 3) tempest, 4) acute, 5) endure, 6) buckle, 7) complex, 10) flawless, 12) extravagant, 13) bald,15) untamed, 16) yacht, 17) alibi, 21) riddle, 24) align, 26) fret, 28) dip, 29) nab

x

Crossword 4 grid:

```
T . . . S . C E A S E
R E D U C E . . U . N
I . . U . . . . N . D
U . C A L A M I T Y
M . O . P . . D . . C
P U N C T U A L . . O
H . C . U . . E . . A
. . U . R . . . C A R
. G R U E S O M E . S
A . . . . T . . D I E
I . . V A G U E
D E F Y . G . . . . F
E . L . B . D . . . R
. . E . L . O . A . A
A N X I O U S . G I G
P . I . U . E . E . R
R O B U S T . . N . A
I . L . E . . . D . N
L I E D . V A C A N T
```

# Crossword 4, Pages 32-33

## Across:

3) Cease, 6) Reduce, 7) Calamity, 10) Punctual,
11) Car, 12) Gruesome, 15) Die, 16) Vague,
17) Defy, 23) Anxious, 24) Gig, 25) Robust, 26) Lied,
27) Vacant

## Down:

1) Triumph, 2) Sculpture, 4) Aunt, 5) End, 7) Concur,
8) Idle, 9) Coarse, 11) Cede, 13) Stag, 14) Aide,
18) Flexible, 19) Fragrant, 20) Blouse, 21) Dose,
22) Agenda, 23) April

# Crossword 5, Pages 34-35

## Across:

1) Omen, 3) Awkward, 6) Carriage,
8) Map, 9) Hid, 11) Dash, 12) Temple,
15) Dolphin, 16) Fascinating, 17) Cosy, 18) Idol,
20) Arrive, 22) Awe, 24) Etc., 25) Easel, 26) Purify

## Down:

1) Orchestra, 2) Earth, 4) Despise, 5) Bird, 7) Gold,
10) Essential, 13) Expensive, 14) Bungalow,
15) Disastrous, 17) Cradle, 19) Omit, 21) Veil,
23) Easy

Crossword 5 grid:

```
O M E N . A W K W A R D
R . A . B . . . . . . E
C A R R I A G E . . . S
H . T . R . . O . M A P
E . H I D . L . E . . I
S . . . . D A S H . . S
T E M P L E . . S . . E
R . . . . X . . E . B
A . D O L P H I N . U
. . I . E . . T . N
F A S C I N A T I N G
. . A . S . . A . A
C O S Y . I D O L . L
R . T . V . M . . O
A R R I V E . I . A W E
D . O . E . T C . . A
L . U . I . . . . . S
E A S E L . P U R I F Y
```

Crossword 6 grid:

```
E A R N . P I E C E . R
N . . . E . L . . . E
T I E . A S C E N D . F
R . X . S . V . R . L
A . A C T I V E . A . E
N . M . M . N . M . C
C . . . I . . F A S T
E . B O A S T . E . I
. . O . T . . A . V
L U X U R I O U S . E
. . E . C . T . C
P U R S E . . . S H Y
A . . A . I . . . A
R E C L U S E . G . N
C . . O . L . J U D G E
H A U N T E D . I . E
E . . O . . . D
D I S C O U R T E O U S
```

# Crossword 6, Pages 36-37

## Across:

1) Earn, 2) Piece, 5) Tie, 7) Ascend, 9) Active
10) Fast, 11) Boast ,12) Luxurious, 14) Purse,
16) Shy, 18) Recluse, 20) Judge, 21) Haunted,
23) Discourteous

## Down:

1) Entrance, 2) Pessimistic, 3) Eleven, 4) Reflective,
6) Exam, 8) Drama, 10) Feast – A banquet
11) Boxer, 13) Change, 14) Parched, 15) Salon,
17) Isle, 19) Guide, 22) Too

## Crossword 7, Pages 38-39

**Across:**

1) Obedient, 4) Aid, 7) Cattle, 8) Roof, 9) Punish, 10) Basic, 13) NE, 14) Trot, 15) Still, 16) Nudge, 17) Awful, 20) Stylish, 22) Raw, 24) Partial, 25) Irate, 26) Gloomy, 29) Delays, 31) Frustrating

**Down:**

1) Occupation, 2) Extend, 3) Elephant, 5) Difficult, 6) Currant, 11) Seizure, 12) Fragile, 15) Sows, 18) ASAP, 19) Chilly, 20) Straight, 21) Brolly, 23) Weak, 27) Mourn, 28) Plot, 30) Sat

```
O B E D I E N T . . A I D
C . X . . L . . C . . I
C A T T L E . . U . . F
U . E . P . . R O O F .
P U N I S H . . R . . I
A . D . A . B A S I C .
T . . F . N . . N E . U
I . T R O T . . S T I L L
O . . A . . . O . Z . T
N U D G E . A W F U L .
. . I . A . S . R . C .
S T Y L I S H . . E . H
T . . E . A . B . . . I
R A W . . P A R T I A L
A . E . . . O . . . L .
I R A T E . G L O O M Y
G . K . . P . L . O . .
H . . D E L A Y S . U .
T . . . . O . . A . R .
. F R U S T R A T I N G
```

## Crossword 8, Pages 40-41

**Across:**

1) Scorching, 6) Rain, 7) Visible, 8) Surf, 9) Gas, 10) Bawl, 13) Far, 15) Oral, 16) Plume, 18) Ran, 19) Gossip, 21) Embrace, 24) Even, 26) Use, 29) Smooth, 31) Task, 32) Ban, 36) Mimic, 37) Bleach, 38) Eager, 40) Odd, 41) Mean, 42) Hungry

**Down:**

1) Savage, 2) Oasis, 3) Hollow, 4) Grasp, 5) Uniform, 11) Arena, 12) Lodge, 13) Flash, 14) Curb, 16) Present, 17) Mar, 20) Pea, 22) Crumb, 23) Neon, 25) Easy, 27) Soar, 28) Chasm, 30) Rancid, 33) Alone, 34) Talon, 35) Shed, 36) Mug, 39) Eon

```
S C O R C H I N G . . U
A . A . . O . . R A I N
V I S I B L E . . A . I
A . I . . L . . S U R F
G A S . . O . . P . . O
E . . B A W L . . F A R
. . C . R . O R A L . M
P L U M E . D . . A . .
R . R A N . G O S S I P
E M B R A C E . . H . E
S . . . R . N . . . A .
E V E N . U S E . . C .
N . A . S M O O T H . R
T A S K . B A N . A . A
. . Y . . R . . . S . N
. A . T . S . M I M I C
B L E A C H . U . . . I
. O . L . E A G E R . D
. N . O D D . . O . . .
M E A N . . H U N G R Y
```

## Anagrams 1, Page 44

1) B. SPARSE, 2) D. PERSIST, 3) A. HARDEST, 4) D. ALERTED, 5) C. EARLY, 6) D. STAKE, 7) B. WORSE, 8) C. PLEAS, 9) A. REWARD, 10) C. SPAN

## Anagrams 2, Page 45

1) DISMAL, 2) MANOR, 3) EMBELLISH, 4) RUPTURE, 5) INCOGNITO, 6) SQUEAL, 7) NOVICE, 8) TABLET, 9) LIVID, 10) FRIGID, 11) ERRATIC, 12) MUGGY

## Anagrams 3, Page 46

1) NOMINAL, 2) AVERAGE, 3) MEDDLE, 4) SULLEN, 5) IMPORTANT, 6) STRUT, 7) DECEPTIVE, 8) DELUSION, 9) REMNANTS, 10) COPSE, 11) PERTURBED, 12) GENUINE, 13) WAIVE, 14) SQUANDER, 15) NEBULOUS

**Anagrams 4, Page 47**

1) MALE – Meal, Lame  2) READ – Dare, Dear  3) TEAM – Mate, Meat, Tame, Meta

4) POLO – Loop, Pool  5) BREAK – Brake, Baker  6) CHARM – March  7) ROUTE – Outer

8) LUMBER – Rumble  9) AMUSES – Assume  10) LISTEN - Silent


**Just for Fun - Word Scramble, Page 48**

HIEROGLYPH, PYRAMID, PHARAOH, SPHINX, SCARAB

Main theme: **Ancient Egypt**


**Compound Words 1, Page 49**

1) C. waterfall,  2) D. tablespoon,  3) B. bargain,  4) C. rainbow,  5) E. underestimate,

6) A. friendship,  7) C. boardwalk,  8) B. Rocketship,  9) E. headband,  10) D. fingernail,

11) D. cartwheel,  12) C. blueberry


**Compound Words 2, Page 50**

1) aeroplane,  2) armchair,  3) toothpaste,  4) horseplay,  5) candlelight,  6) bodyguard,

7) bookstore,  8) handshake,  9) newspaper,  10) mainstream,  11) highlight,  12) shoelace


**Compound Words 3, Page 51**

1) noteworthy,  2) brainwash,  3) proofread,  4) nightfall,  5) timeline,  6) extraordinary,

7) wrongdoing,  8) commonwealth  9) fortnight,  10) hereafter,  11) layover,  12) tailbone


**Spreading the Word -1, Page 52**

1) adopt,  2) aloof,  3) consist,  4) occur,  5) bleak,  6) glib,  7) fatal,  8) suspend,  9) curb,
10) sage


**Spreading the Word -2, Page 53**

1) ally,  2) unkempt,  3) hinder,  4) sermon,  5) devote,  6) lament,  7) allay,  8) heed,  9) risqué,
10) serene,  11) lunar,  12) vain


**Spreading the Word -3, Page 54**

1) rowdy,  2) liable,  3) coax,  4) rogue,  5) mere,  6) repent,  7) linger,  8) odour,  9) traitor,
10) tenant,  11) compel,  12) peril

**Just for Fun – Cloze Word Search,**

**Page 55**

1) Camping,  2) Sunglasses,

3) Passport,  4) Sunscreen,

5) Backpack, 6) Lido,  7) Hotel,

8) Luggage, 9) Postcard,  10) Tourist

```
B U S I D R A C T S O P B
A K M U Y N I P A S S C A
R C S U N S C R E E N L C
M A P A K G N I P M A C K
C P C R T E L A E L T E L
A K G O E G S A R D O T H
R C U P A S S E S G L O S
D A D E P T A L G S T I W
E B T O U R I S T E E J P
G O R A S O D I L A O S Q
A T I H L U G G A G E B L
```

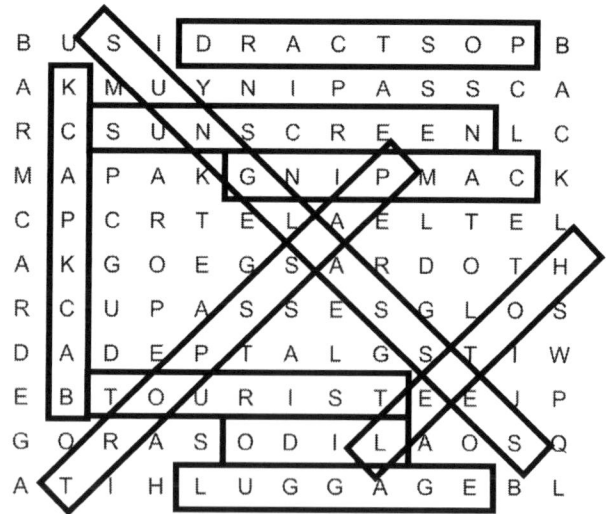

## Connections 1, Page 56

1) uniform,  2) gorge,  3) current,  4) band,  5) bowl,  6) bright,  7) well,  8) lie,  9) bark,
10) console

## Connections 2, Page 57

1) current,  2) contest,  3) spring,  4) mode,  5) intrigue,  6) funny,  7) firm,  8) pretty,  9) contract,
10) engage

## Connections 3, Page 58

1) relish,  2) mark,  3) hard,  4) address, 5) bar,  6) ball,  7) grave,  8) model,  9) attribute,
10) discount

## Connections 4, Page 59

1) spot,  2) rule,  3) gift,  4) block,  5) part,  6) bluff,  7) column,  8) channel,  9) field,  10) coach

## Odd One Out 1, Page 60

1) football,  2) rock,  3) read,  4) complex,  5) disturbing,  6) swimming,  7) spear,  8) broad,
9) friend,  10) apple

## Odd One Out 2, Page 61

1) minuscule,  2) zucchini, 3) native,  4) scarf,  5) impractical,  6) shadow,  7) number,
8) trickery,  9) contemporary,  10) history,  11) computer (others are round),  12) profound

## Odd One Out 3, Page 62

1) selection,  2) bicycle,  3) fortunate,  4) tank,  5) table,  6) cheese,  7) compass,  8) ambiguous,
9) glacial,  10) parka, 11) kiosk  12) pare

## Odd One Out 4, Page 63

1) abdomen, 2) potent, 3) bland, 4) baffled, 5) antenna, 6) unsophisticated, 7) cube,

8) mesmerised, 9) savour, 10) lopsided, 11) pencil, 12) emit

## Odd One Out 5, Page 64

1) reconciliation, 2) oblivion, 3) toil, 4) patron, 5) dictionary, 6) matches (not a compound

word), 7) enduring, 8) mandarin (does not have a stone), 9) stall, 10) capitulate, 11) union,

12) belt (all of the others have two vowels)

## Just for Fun – Word Scramble, Page 65

Answers: Longitude, scale, river, map north

Main theme – GEOGRAPHY

## Just for Fun – Rebus Puzzles, Pages 66-69

1) Long time no see (Long time – no 'c')

2) Elbow ('bow' in L shape)

3) Good afternoon

4) For once in my life (four 1's in 'my life')

5) Foreign language (The letter n 4 times in language)

6) Who's in charge? (The word 'who' twice in the word 'charge')

7) You're under arrest

8) Seasoning (c's on ing)

9) Dancing in the rain

10) Too intense (two in 10's)

11) Get in touch

12) Someone is following me

13) Summary (sum of Mary + Mary)

14) Belly (Bell + y)

15) Benign (B-9)

16) Tenacity (10 + a + city)

17) Exorbitant (X + orbit + ant)

18) Paradox (A pair of docs)

19) Robust (row + bust)

20) Inspire (N + spire)

21) Abundance (A + bun + dance)

22) Hint (H in T)

23) X-Ray (x on a sting ray)

24) Ice Cream (I screaming)

25) Neon light (Knee on light)

26) Foul Language (quack gobble squawk cluck honk)

27) Comfortable (com + four tables)

28) Low Key

29) The stakes (steaks) are high

30) Mood swing

31) Epic (e + pick)

32) Seal of approval

**Complete the Word 1, Page 70**

1) goldfish, 2) believe, 3) despite, 4) followed, 5) shutters, 6) apply, 7) cupboard, 8) minor, 9) wooden, 10) subscription

**Complete the Word 2, Page 71**

1) appeared, 2) podcasts, 3) rumour, 4) below, 5) competition, 6) chemistry, 7) surroundings, 8) frugal, 9) sustainable, 10) tapestry, 11) pyramids, 12) contributed

**Complete the Word 3, Page 72**

1) flourish, 2) adjourned, 3) ambiguous, 4) convince, 5) flamboyant, 6) exasperated, 7) potential, 8) transparent, 9) managed, 10) grotesque, 11) appealed, 12) armoured

**Complete the Word 4, Page 73**

1) condone, 2) forlorn, 3) finesse, 4) raging, 5) arduous, 6) element, 7) crowds, 8) compete, 9) ambition, 10) notice, 11) anecdote, 12) indignant

**Complete the Word 5, Page 74**

1) irreverent, 2) leisurely, 3) prominent, 4) prolong, 5) defend, 6) apathetic, 7) sedentary, 8) nauseating, 9) extended, 10) bickering, 11) confined, 12) residence

**Just for Fun – Cloze Word Search, Page 76**

1) aroma, 2) cacophony, 3) murky, 4) pungent, 5) coarse, 6) spicy, 7) damp, 8) vivid

What do these words relate to? **SENSES**

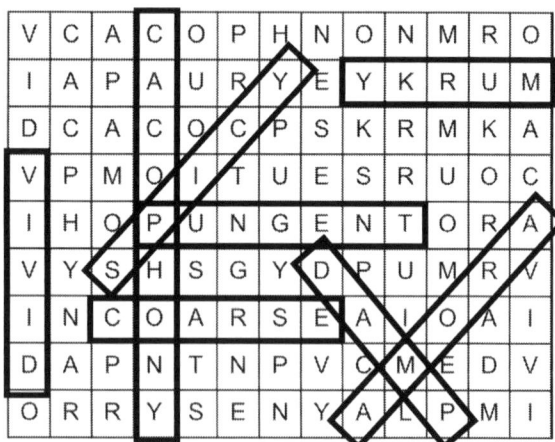

**Missing Letter Sentences 1, Page 77**

1) example, 2) visited, 3) decided, 4) Famous, 5) exercise, 6) training, 7) opposite, 8) shame, 9) favourite, 10) their, 11) choose, 12) sight, 13) climate, 14) imagine, 15) camera

**Missing Letter Sentences 2, Page 78**

1) dreamt, 2) quality, 3) reach, 4) taste, 5) theatre, 6) prize, 7) broken, 8) Catch, 9) Which, 10) amusement, 11) moment, 12) Nobody, 13) picture, 14) lifted, 15) around

## Missing Letter Sentences 3, Page 79

1) every, 2) pointed, 3) type, 4) sure, 5) beautiful, 6) Sharp, 7) steep, 8) proud, 9) special,

10) large, 11) spacecraft, 12) journey, 13) author, 14) gardening, 15) spread

## Missing Letter Sentences 4, Page 80

1) restore, 2) novel, 3) barge, 4) pitch, 5) defect, 6) vane, 7) phobia, 8) murky, 9) Dial,

10) severe, 11) stomach, 12) neon, 13) nimble, 14) alter, 15) compass

## Missing Letter Sentences 5, Page 81

1) width, 2) distinguishing, 3) swarm, 4) industry, 5) Jewellery, 6) cellar, 7) faint, 8) banquets,

9) temperature, 10) amphibians, 11) bunting, 12) priceless, 13) Consult, 14) Sleet, 15) fleet

## Missing Letter Sentences 6, Page 82

1) Fetch, 2) reigned, 3) rural, 4) dusk, 5) rhythm, 6) extremely, 7) tomatoes, 8) necessary,

9) Popular, 10) audience, 11) enough, 12) unusual, 13) leopard, 14) mountain, 15) terminal

## Missing Letter Sentences 7, Page 83

1) abundance, 2) apprehensive, 3) dismal, 4) director, 5) helix, 6) lavish, 7) orthodontist,

8) perplexed, 9) resort, 10) uniform, 11) wound, 12) dwellings, 13) alert, 14) benefit,

15) charred

## Missing Letter Sentences 8, Page 84

1) deliberate, 2) demolished, 3) emerged, 4) humble, 5) Trivia, 6) slope, 7) obscure,

8) contract, 9) flee, 10) drought, 11) habitats, 12) antiques, 13) summit, 14) Sturdy,

15) extinction

## Missing Letter Sentences 9, Page 85

1) tranquil, 2) tormented, 3) pulled, 4) kerb, 5) taught, 6) loot, 7) trough, 8) restore,

9) article, 10) plumber, 11) alibi, 12) cast 13) firm, 14) platt, 15) feline

## Just For Fun – Cloze Word Search, Page 86

1) Gravity, 2) Star, 3) Constellation,
4) Telescope, 5) Comet, 6) Asteroid,
7) Universe, 8) Pluto

Theme : **Astronomy**

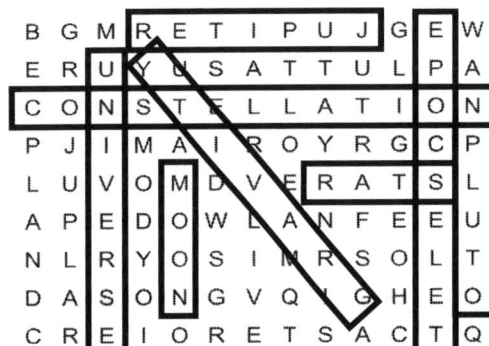

**Just for Fun – Word Themes, Page 87**

<u>Department Store</u>: apparel, blazer, escalator,  jewellery, textiles

<u>Doctor's Surgery</u>: antiseptic, diagnosis, gauze, stethoscope

<u>Education</u>: curriculum, lecture, literacy, rubber, whiteboard

<u>Restaurant</u>: appetiser, cuisine, entrée, savoury

<u>Ironmonger</u>: hardware, hinges, tools, utensils

**Missing Words 1, Page 88**

1) terminal   2) composer   3) sombre   4) obscured   5) swell, violet   6) chords   7) volatile
8) sauntered   9) jovial, prosperous   10) draft   11) lethargic   12) distress   13) forecast
14)  thaw   15) drab   16) sabre

**Missing Words 2, Page 89**

1) barge, cargo   2) artifacts, globe   3) support   4) chevron, decorating
5) clothing, strewn   6) orchard, bare   7) alibi, released   8) friar, dense   9) source, reservoir
10) elapsed, generation   11) coax, nervous   12) forgo, embarked

**Missing Words 3, Page 90**

1) generous, sponsored   2) current, reliant   3) dainty, distracted   4) chilly, gloomy
5) extracted, fragile   6) meagre, pondered   7) biased, reverse   8) solution, opposite
9) courteous, obedient   10) aimlessly, yearned   11) cultures, errors   12) faint, adjust

**Missing Words 4, Page 91**

1) thrifty, mend   2) capital, ancient   3) boisterous, engaged   4) diluted, strength
5) hostile, rigid   6) hamper, descent   7) humid, exotic   8) occupation, witty
9) revealed, innocent   10) delicate, desirable   11) mesmerising, perplexing
12) aloof, callous

**Missing Words 5, Page 92**

1) hapless, disastrous   2) debris, vapour   3) assortment, nourishment   4) investigate, prominent
5) complimented, portrait   6) complemented, crumble   7) entertained, illusions
8) lenient, remorse   9) dwelling, quaint   10) apprentice, forthcoming   11) collision, congestion
12) prohibited, enclosures

**Just For Fun – Word Scramble, Page 93**

CHINA, CUTLERY, MATCHES, COLANDER, CLOCK;  Where you might find them – KITCHEN

## Cloze Passages

### Heathrow Airport, Page 95

1) kilometres, 2) Europe, 3) regional, 4) renamed, 5) hamlet, 6) operation, 7) affordable, 8) handling, 9) currently, 10) longest, 11) terminals, 12) dedicated, 13) runways, 14) debate, 15) Gatwick

### Unicorns, Page 96

1) mythical, 2) spiralling, 3) reputation, 4) originated, 5) ancient, 6) tapestries, 7) portrayed, 8) purity, 9) healing, 10) symbol, 11) depicted, 12) representative, 13) association, 14) accessible, 15) refer

### Edinburgh, Page 97

1) cultural, 2) destination, 3) inhabited, 4) events, 5) united, 6) seat, 7) focal, 8) series, 9) residence, 10) spacious, 11) insurance, 12) industries, 13) nicknamed, 14) beacon, 15) graduates

### Cheltenham Literature Festival, Page 98

1) guests, 2) recognised, 3) oldest, 4) attracts, 5) spoken, 6) debates, 7) range 8) primarily, 9) venues, 10) location, 11) affords, 12) there, 13) workshops, 14) pandemic, 15) acclaim

### The Praying Mantis, Page 99

1) front, 2) fearsome, 3) prey, 4) help, 5) including, 6) cannibalise, 7) odd, 8) set, 9) develop, 10) vary, 11) mimic, 12) unlikely, 13) encounter, 14) accidentally, 15) migrating, 16) spread

### Rio de Janeiro, Page 100

1) backdrop, 2) explorers, 3) mistake , 4) empire, 5) independence, 6) attraction, 7) observance, 8) evolved 9) dancers, 10) iconic, 11) peak, 12) South, 13) their, 14) tropical

### Call of the Wild, Pages 101-102

Expose – protect, departed – approached, straightened – wound, front – rear, poky – spacious, columns – rows, chaotic – orderly, deserted – populous, clearly – obscurely, entrance – recesses, usually – rarely, abandoned – escorted, tame – wild, meekly – imperiously, partially – utterly, disconnected – inseparable, limited – universal

**Millicent Fawcett, Pages 103-104**

Unfaithful – committed, briefly – tirelessly, apathetic – devoted, dispersed – organised, dissuaded – encouraged, violent – peaceful, conformed – contrasted, harmony – disobedience, separating – aligning, insignificant – major, combatants – pacifists, peace – conflict, closed – extended, sedentary – active, disgraced – honoured

**Just for Fun – Animal Scramble, Page 105**

1) Badger,  2) Hedgehog,  3) Lobster,  4) Dolphin,  5) Giraffe,  6) Jaguar,  7) Hamster,
8) Kangaroo,  9) Parrot,  10)  Gorilla

**Just For Fun – Word Ladders, Pages 106-107**

CAT – HAT – HOT – HOG – DOG
FAIR – FAIL – SAIL – SOIL – SOUL – FOUL
TRICK – THICK – CHICK – CHECK – CHEEK – CREEK – CREED – BREED – BREAD – TREAD – TREAT
PAPER – TAPER – TAPES – TAKES – CAKES – CASES –CASTS – COSTS – COATS – CHATS – CHAPS – CLAPS – CLASS -GLASS
NOSIY – NOISE – POISE – PRISE – PRIME – CRIME – CLIME – SLIME – SLIDE – GLIDE – GUIDE – GUILE – GUILT – QUILT - QUIET

**Jumbled Sentences 1, Pages 108-110**

1) A. (Isaac did not like to read crime novels.)

2) A. (We had a satisfying lunch in the new café.)

3) C. (The council decided to close the park because it was unsafe.)

4) B. (Dad was expecting a parcel to arrive at any moment.)

5) C. (Welsh is a language that is still spoken in Wales today.)

6) A. (The longest river in the United Kingdom is the River Severn.)

7) C. (The man's calm nature helped to quickly settle the disagreement.)

8) B. (Hot chocolate is my favourite indulgence.)

9) C. (Gerry just bought an expensive sports car.)

10) A. (In desperate times, the troops showed true courage.)

11) B.(The idea of hiking in a thunderstorm was sheer madness.)

12) A. (Both nations agreed to the treaty in principle.)

13) C. (The company's workers were their greatest asset.)

14) B. (The pilot went to inspect his aeroplane in the hangar.)

15) B. (Gina was successful in launching her new clothing line.)

**Jumbled Sentences 1, Pages 108-110 (continued)**

16) A. (The eminent physicist won the Nobel Prize.)

17) A. (The professor's lecture on Shakespeare was interesting.)

18) B. (Nico made a dangerous journey to London.)

19) B. (Freddie came home at approximately 6:00 p.m.)

**Jumbled Sentences 2, Pages 111-112**

1) B. hydrated (Unless it rains soon, the crops will be devastated.)

2) A. frustrating (Winning the competition was a gratifying experience.)

3) C. complicated (Unlike his brother, Jules did not make friends easily.)

4) A. designate (Cedric had grandiose plans to build a castle.)

5) C. achievement (The organist made a mistake and played the wrong hymn.)

6) B. debated (Alberto agreed to the contract without any amendments.)

7) B. fewer (During the pandemic, in-person events became less common.)

8) A. meeting (Martin would not say with whom he had met.)

9) C. employed (Alice enjoyed her part-time job at the cinema.)

10) A. integrated (We need more leaders with integrity.)

**Jumbled Sentences 3, Pages 113-114**

1) B. (The children ran into an open field.)

2) C. (It was his ambition to attend university and become a doctor.)

3) B. (Vegetables grow best in fertile soil.)

4) A. (The designer was known for his colourful and flamboyant clothing.)

5) B. (Unfortunately, we had to stay in a shabby hotel.)

6) C. (An emergency was declared after the flooding.)

7) A. (The boy was nimble and easily navigated the obstacle.)

8) B. (The loud noise outside affected their ability to concentrate.)

9) A. (Mark had a bad conscience about making her do all the work.)

10) B. (Henry was always in trouble for improperly wearing his school uniform.)

**Jumbled Sentences 4, Pages 115-116**

1) C. dessert (Mum's favourite dessert is strawberry ice cream.)

2) A. band (We don't know when the band will be performing tonight.)

3) C. ruins (Our climb to the summit of Snowdonia was not spoiled by bad weather.)

4) A. feature (Gemma's smartphone has a feature that shares her location.)

### Jumbled Sentences 4, Pages 115-116 (Continued)

5) A. bewildered  (Davey was bewildered by the number of choices.)

6) B. brought  (Brian always brought a water bottle to school.)

7) D. good  (Finding a good electrician can be challenging.)

8) B. an  (I received an email from my cousin in Canada.)

9) C. wide  (The convenience store sells a wide variety of sweets.)

10) C. thrive  (The mice seem to thrive in the abandoned house.)

### Jumbled Sentences 5, Pages 117-118

1) C – B – E – A – D

2) E – B – D – C – A

3) D – A – E – B – C

4) D – B – E – C –A

5) A – G – D – B – E – C – F

6) B – A – D – C

7) D – B – A – E – G – F – C

8) D – B – C – E – A

### Analogies 1, Page 119

1) cat, horse  2) night, left  3) book, hand  4) row, sweep  5) learning, fitness  6) hospital, hotel

7) desert, storm  8) dairy, poultry  9) close, together  10) 1000, 10  11) head, foot  12) orchard, library

### Analogies 2, Page 120

1) confidence, happiness  2) paper, sweater  3) aeroplane, car  4) bakery, café  5) storm, blizzard

6) pachyderm, feline  7) help, obstruct  8) classroom, orchestra  9) paw, hoof  10) whole, origin

11) maps, words  12) freeze, boil

### Analogies 3, Page 121

1) computer, trousers  2) amphibian, media  3) envelope, shell  4) fruit, vegetable

5) construction,  sculpture  6) for, pair (both are homophones)  7) food, water  8) foe, friend

9) scream, whisper  10) currency, book  11) turncoat, wit  12) oppose, serious

### Just for Fun – River Crossing, Page 122

Across the river: help – aid – serve – rescue;

Back to safety:  refuge – sanctuary – shelter – immunity

### What is True? Page 123

1) b  (Felicity is 12, John is 10, Emma is 8, Billy is 7.)

2) d  (All of the others have been to 4 countries)

**Move a Letter, Page 124**

1) A – live, read  2) L – food, clap  3) R – bake, rare  4) U – case, found  5) E – pace, tape

6) C – sale, cape  7) R – fist, tree  8) H – tough, hedge  9) S – desert, self  10) A – lunch, relay

11) P – irate, rapid  12) N – violet, narrow


**Rearranging Letters, Page 125**

1) b. hack  2) c. pact  3) d. fake  4) a. twin  5) d. home  6) c. only  7) b. epic  8) c. tuba


**Alphabet Code, Page 126**

1) d. OQ  2) b. IY  3) a. HL  4) c. UT  5) b. LN  6) c. SW  7) d. VW  8) b. BD


**Alphabet Code 2, Page 127**

1) b. MO  2) d. JL  3) a. PR  4) e. MJ  5) c. ST  6) b. JM  7) c. TT  8) e. ST


**Alphabet Code 3, Page 128**

1) a. VWRS  2) c. IWCLEA  3) e. TWFSLJ  4) b. BUS  5) d. GIANT  6) a. BLIP


**Answers to Symbols, Page 176**

1) Thumbs up – everything's good,  2) WIFI (Wireless),  3) Hazard/Warning,  4) Barber,

5) Recycling,  6) Peace,  7) Euro,  8) Dollar,  9) Infinity,  10) Power on button


**Spelling Test 1, Page 182**

1) their,  2) whether,  3) lose,  4) stationary,  5) principle,  6) effect,  7) sheared,  8) ascended,

9) flair,  10) There,  11) prise,  12) weak,  13) Except,  14) affected,  15) loose,  16) prayed,

17) hangers,  18) principal,  19) bare,  20) accept


**Spelling Test 2, Page 183**

1) accommodate,  2) awkward,  3) twelfth,  4) maintenance,  5) disappointed,  6) autumn,

7) humorous,  8) foreign,  9) pigeon,  10) guarantee


**Spelling Test 3, Page 184**

1) chaos,  2) jewellery,  3) reign,  4) symbol,  5) novel,  6) compliment,  7) interrupt,

8) faithfully,  9) collision,  10) ancient

**Spelling Test 4, Page 185**

1) aerial, 2) destroy, 3) committee, 4) handkerchief, 5) miniature, 6) accidentally, 7) queue, 8) accepted, 9) vacuum, 10) generally

**Spelling Test 5, Page 186**

1) February, 2) marvellous, 3) accompany, 4) mischievous, 5) stomach, 6) environment, 7) weight, 8) believe, 9) description, 10) doubt

**Spelling Test 6, Page 187**

1) dreamt, 2) quay, 3) advice, 4) Egypt, 5) occur, 6) unusual, 7) possession, 8) irritable, 9) counterfeit, 10) absence

**Spelling Test 7, Page 188**

1) bruise, 2) discipline, 3) harass, 4) persuade, 5) skilful, 6) manouvre, 7) category, 8) extremely, 9) laugh, 10) noticeable

**Spelling Test 8, Page 189**

1) muscle, 2) separate, 3) acquaintance, 4) cemetery 5) leisure, 6) occasion, 7) calendar, 8) scissors, 9) thorough, 10) acknowledge

# Also available from the Armadillo's Pillow:

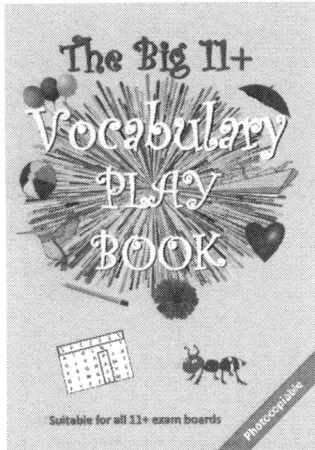

### The Big 11+ Vocabulary Play Book

A fun and engaging way to learn over 1,000 words for the Eleven Plus Exam. Includes games, puzzles, cartoons, quizzes, rhymes and tongue twisters that address synonym, antonym, analogy, cloze and category questions in a lively way.

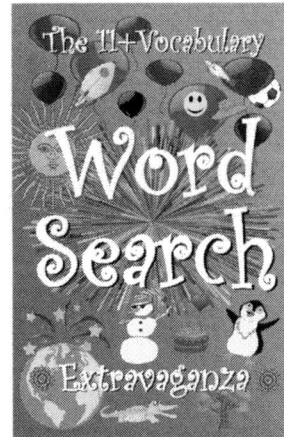

### The 11+ Vocabulary Word Search

A unique word search puzzle book specifically targeting key Eleven Plus vocabulary. Selected Eleven Plus topic areas including synonyms and antonyms, maths, shapes, landscapes, animals, buildings, and many more.

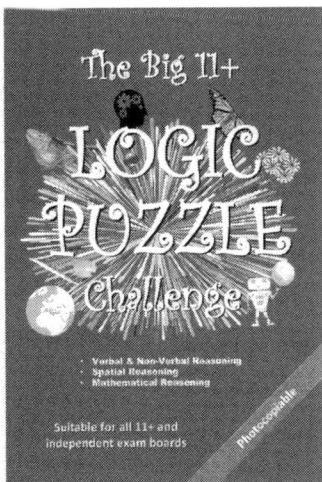

### The Big 11+ Logic Puzzle Extravaganza

A unique collection of logic puzzles including worded problems, spatial reasoning, cube nets and more. Excellent for additional verbal and non-verbal reasoning practice.

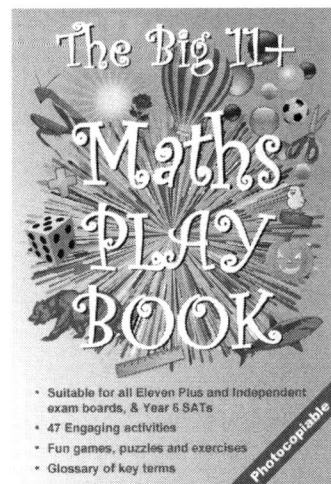

### The Big 11+ Maths Play Book

47 engaging activities, including games, puzzles, cartoons, and exercises that address key Eleven Plus Maths subject areas in a lively way.

For bulk orders, questions or comments, please contact us at: thearmadillospillow@gmail.com

Printed in Great Britain
by Amazon